ASIAN FLAVORS

ASIAN FLAVORS

UNLOCK CULINARY SECRETS WITH SPICES, SAUCES, AND OTHER EXOTIC INGREDIENTS

WENDY SWEETSER

KODANSHA INTERNATIONAL
NEW YORK   TOKYO   LONDON

A QUINTET BOOK

Published in 2005 by Kodansha America, Inc.
Kodansha America, Inc.
575 Lexington Avenue, New York, NY 10022, USA

Kodansha International Ltd.
17–14 Otowa 1-chome, Bunkyo-ku, Tokyo 112-8652, Japan

Library of Congress Cataloging-in-Publication Data

Sweetser, Wendy.
Asian flavors: unlock culinary secrets with spices, sauces, and other
exotic ingredients / Wendy Sweetser.
        p. cm.
   Includes index.
    ISBN-13: 978-1-56836-359-2
    ISBN-10: 1-56836-359-1 (pbk.)
   1. Cookery, Asian.   I. Title.
TX724.5.A1S94 2005
641.595—dc22   2005043411

This book was designed and produced by
Quintet Publishing Limited
6 Blundell Street
London N7 9BH

Project Editor Ruth Patrick
Editors Catherine Osborne, Jenny Doubt
Art Director Roland Codd
Food Stylist Wendy Sweetser
Photographer Ian Garlick
Publisher Ian Castello-Cortes

Manufactured in Singapore by Pica Digital Pte Ltd.
Printed in China by SNP Leefung Printers Ltd.
9 8 7 6 5 4 3 2 1

Picture Credits Getty Images p6, p9

CONTENTS

INTRODUCTION

All cuisines have certain ingredients and flavors that set them apart and make them special, but nowhere is this more apparent than in Southeast Asia. Ginger, lemon grass, Thai basil, coconut, and chiles are just a few of the tempting aromas and seasonings that seduce when you go out for an Asian meal. Take a stroll through a food market in Thailand, Hong Kong, Vietnam, or your local Chinatown, and you'll be dazzled by the colorful array of fresh fruit, vegetables, and herbs that local cooks take for granted.

In this book, I explore ten different flavors that, more than any others, define Asian food for me. Many and varied, they all play an equally important part in Far Eastern kitchens where, unlike many of us in the West, cooks are content to use the same foods they have grown and harvested for thousands of years rather than seek out the latest must-have ingredient.

Lightly cooked dishes made with the freshest produce are the hallmark of Asian cuisines—"fast food" is the norm. Not the pre-prepared microwave variety, or the kind which is delivered to your door, but dishes made with ingredients that are quickly prepared and rapidly cooked to share with family and friends.

Down the centuries foreign settlers have left their mark on Asia's many and varied cultures but their influences have been allowed to merge into and become part of a local cuisine rather than fundamentally change it. Go out for a street food lunch in Saigon and you'll see baguettes piled high on food stalls alongside the hawkers stirring pots of bo kho, the local spicy beef stew. Creamy cakes and desserts became part of Indonesian cuisine through the influence of the Dutch, and tomatoes, olives, and paella found their way into Filipino kitchens when the Spanish arrived on their shores.

Although many Asian countries have "signature" dishes such as Thailand's green curry, Hong Kong's sweet and sour pork, and Japanese sukiyaki, you are likely to find as many variations of those dishes as people cooking them. Sauces, spice mixes, and dressings are complex creations in their own right, closely guarded family recipes are passed onto the next generation and, as a rule, little is written down. Every small culinary masterpiece is achieved by tasting, tasting, and more tasting as the chef strives to get the balance of flavors exactly right.

Asian people love to eat but that love is not a simple craving for food. They see a meal as an opportunity to celebrate sitting down with family and friends and sharing the good things in life. In this book I have sought to capture the essence of Asian flavors through some of the best recipes I've accumulated and developed myself over the years. Asian food is all about sharing, so next time you plan to entertain, prepare a selection of your favorite dishes and lay them out with pride on the table for your guests to enjoy. In Asia they say a good meal should start well and continue to a memorable finish. If I can tempt you to try your hand at discovering just some of the enticing flavors from the East, I promise you won't be disappointed.

LEFT This spice stall in a market in Bangkok, Thailand shows the variety of herbs and spices typically on offer.

GLOSSARY

BEAN CURD / TOFU
Known as bean curd in China and tofu in Japan, this is made from the milky liquid that drains out of crushed soy beans. The liquid is coagulated and pressed in a process similar to cheesemaking. Available in blocks as soft, firm, silken, or smoked, the silken style has a more acidic flavor and slightly firmer texture than soft.

DRIED CHINESE MUSHROOMS
Dried Chinese mushrooms such as cloud ear fungus or black mushrooms are available from Asian stores. In their dried state they can be stored indefinitely in a cool, dry place but need to be soaked in warm water before cooking. The soaking water can be used as stock but should be strained through a fine sieve to remove any grit that may have become trapped in the mushrooms.

EDAMAME BEANS
The Japanese name for the green soy bean, available fresh or frozen. Boil the beans in their pods in a pan of boiling water until just tender, then pop them out and add them to soups, sauces, and salads.

EGGPLANT
Four varieties of eggplant are used in Thai cuisine, two that feel soft when pressed and two that are hard. The two soft ones are the large purple-skinned eggplant popular in Mediterranean cooking and a long, thin, pale purple skinned variety. The two hard ones are the pea eggplant, which is sold on the stalk and resembles large green berries, and a round variety, the size of a small egg, that ranges from creamy white to pale green in colour.

ENOKI MUSHROOMS
Creamy white mushrooms with tiny caps and long, thin stalks. A popular addition to Japanese soups, enoki mushrooms are sold in a bunch with their roots still attached to keep them fresh. Snip off just above the root with scissors and only lightly cook so the mushrooms retain their crunchy texture and slightly fruity flavor.

GREEN AND BLACK TEAS
More delicately flavored than black tea, green tea is made by simply drying the freshly picked leaves of the tea plant. With black tea, the leaves are wilted and then left to ferment so they oxidise before being dried.

LOTUS ROOT
The root of the Chinese lotus or water lily, which grows in lakes and ponds. After harvesting during the late summer and fall, the seeds are eaten as a snack or ground into a sweet paste as a filling for cakes and buns. The root has a crunchy texture and attractive lace-like appearance and, when sliced, can be stir-fried or steamed as a vegetable and deep-fried as a snack. The light reddish-brown skin should be peeled away before slicing.

NORI SEAWEED
Used for making rolled sushi, yaki-nori is toasted seaweed and is available in sheets in packets from Japanese stores. Once a pack is opened the sheets should be stored in an airtight container in a cool, dry place.

POMELO
A citrus fruit native to Malaysia and similar to a large grapefruit but with drier flesh. It can be eaten on its own or peeled and segemented and added to salads.

SHIITAKE MUSHROOMS
Widely used in Oriental cuisines, particularly Japanese, these are available fresh or dried and have a unique earthy flavor and meaty texture. The stalks can be tough, so trim with a sharp knife before cooking.

STAR ANISE
A flower-shaped, dark brown seed pod with an aniseed flavor from a tree of the magnolia family. One of the most popular spices in Chinese cuisine, it is used whole or broken into small pieces to add to marinades, sauces, and desserts. It is also ground and mixed with cinnamon, fennel, Szechuan pepper, and cloves to make Chinese five-spice seasoning.

SZECHUAN PEPPER
A round reddish-brown berry that grows on a spiny bush mainly in western China. It is similar to black pepper but with a more aromatic fragrance and mellow flavor.

SHIMEJI MUSHROOMS
Members of the oyster mushroom family, these small to medium-sized mushrooms have a nutty flavor and are used widely in Japanese dishes.

STRAW MUSHROOMS
Native to China, straw mushrooms are widely cultivated in the south of the country on beds of rice straw, hence their name. Small with oval caps, they can be bought in cans from Chinese food stores.

SUSHI-GRADE FISH
When making sushi, sashimi or any other dish using raw fish, it is imperative that the fish is very fresh and of the finest quality. Suitable varieties such as tuna and salmon can be bought from Japanese stores or high quality fishmongers and will be marked "sushi-grade."

TAMARIND
The bean-shaped fruit of the tamarind tree. Available in sticky, dark brown blocks as a pulp or in jars as a paste. The pulp needs soaking in a little boiling water and then straining before use. Tamarind adds a sour, slightly acidic flavor to dishes such as curries.

TURMERIC
Used frequently in curry mixes, turmeric is a rhizome that looks similar to ginger but is smaller. Ground to a powder, it gives dishes a golden hue, but should be used with care as it can stain clothes. The spice has a mild, earthy flavor and is prized for its digestive and antiseptic powers.

WASABI
Fiery, green Japanese horseradish, available as a powder or paste. The paste is usually sold in a tube from which it is squeezed directly onto serving plates as a condiment to accompany sushi and sashimi.

HINTS AND TIPS

USING CHILIES
If you add too much chili to a dish, you can cool the fire in your mouth by eating plain boiled rice or fresh cucumber. When preparing chilies, take care to protect your hands either by wearing rubber gloves or by washing your hands thoroughly in cold water afterwards, especially if you have any small cuts or grazes. Never touch your face or eyes when handling chilies as they can give nasty stinging burns.

WHICH OIL?
In most of the recipes I have specified the use of peanut oil for frying as this is most commonly used in Asian countries, but other mild-flavored oils such as vegetable, soy, or corn oil would be equally suitable. Coconut oil has a high smoke point and is frequently used in Indonesian cuisine. Olive oil, particularly extra virgin olive oil, has too distinct and strong a flavor and is therefore not suitable for Asian recipes.

SEASONING
Many of us now prefer to limit our salt intake for health reasons so, except in one or two instances where it is an integral part of the dish, I have not suggested adding salt. Individual cooks can decide for themselves if a dish requires extra seasoning to suit their taste but soy sauce, fish sauce, and many other Asian ingredients already add a salty flavor, and many will find it is therefore not necessary to add more salt. If you are worried about the salt level of soy sauce, look for low sodium versions of the traditional sauce in stores selling Asian foods, and substitute this if you prefer.

FRESH, BOTTLED, OR CANNED?
Several of the ingredients used in this book can be bought in different forms such as lemon grass and ginger, both of which are available fresh or as a ready-made puree. Where the fresh ingredient is important to the finished dish, we have suggested using it, but in most other cases use whichever form of the ingredient you have available.

CHILI FLOWERS
To make a chili flower to garnish a dish like the one on page 140, make cuts as close together as possible through the pointed end of a chili using a scalpel or small sharp knife and slice about two-thirds down the length of the chili. Leave in a bowl of iced water for several hours in the refrigerator for the "petals" to open.

GINGER & GALANGAL

Ginger is a root that needs to be peeled and grated or sliced fine before it can be added to a dish. Available fresh, pureed, dried, or ground to a powder, it is one of the most commonly used ingredients in Asian cuisines. Pickled red or pink ginger is used to flavor Japanese dishes, particularly sushi. Galangal is a member of the ginger family and has a similar flavor. As with ginger, its tough outer skin needs to be peeled away before the rhizome is grated or sliced. Look for young, pinkish roots as they are fresh and have the best flavor.

FRAGRANT GINGER CHICKEN WITH NOODLES

SERVES 4 · PREPARATION: 15 MINUTES · COOKING: 15 MINUTES

1 tbsp peanut oil

1 medium carrot, cut into sticks

1 green bell pepper, seeded and chopped

4 oz shiitake mushrooms, quartered

2 boneless chicken breasts, skinned and chopped

1³/₄ cups chicken broth

2 tbsp tomato puree or ketchup

2 tbsp light soy sauce

1 tsp fresh ginger puree

4 oz dried medium egg noodles

If you have any leftover cooked chicken, this recipe is a good way to use it up. Chicken that is already cooked won't need stir-frying, so omit step no. 2 and add it with the noodles so it can heat through thoroughly.

1   Heat the oil in a wok and stir-fry the carrot, green bell pepper, and shiitake mushrooms for three minutes.

2   Add the chicken and stir-fry for a further three minutes.

3   Pour in the broth and add the puree or ketchup, light soy sauce, and ginger puree and bring to a simmer.

4   Break the noodles into short lengths and add to the wok, pushing the noodles down so they are immersed in the cooking liquid.

5   Simmer for a further five minutes, or until the noodles are tender. Garnish with cilantro sprigs and serve immediately.

JAPAN

SEARED COD WITH GALANGAL SAUCE

SERVES 4 · PREPARATION: 15 MINUTES · COOKING: 15 MINUTES

5 oz edamame beans
  in their pods
3 tbsp peanut oil
Four 5-oz cod steaks
2 tbsp all-purpose flour
Small knob of fresh
  galangal, peeled and cut
  into thin strips
5 oz shiitake mushrooms
2 tbsp light soy sauce
1 tsp cornstarch
$^3/_4$ cup fish broth
$^1/_2$ red chili, seeded and
  sliced fine

In the West, the green soy beans known as edamame beans are usually sold frozen in their pods. Available in Japanese food stores, they need to be cooked first and then removed from their pods before adding to the sauce.

1   Cook the edamame beans in a saucepan of boiling water for five minutes. Drain and when cool enough to handle, pop the beans out of their pods.

2   Heat 2 tablespoons of peanut oil in a heavy skillet, dust the cod steaks with flour, and sear them for two to three minutes on each side until just cooked. Remove from the pan and keep warm.

3   Add the remaining peanut oil to the skillet and sauté the galangal and shiitake mushrooms for two minutes. Add the soy sauce, mix the cornstarch with a little of the broth until smooth, and stir in with the rest of the broth.

4   Add the chili and edamame beans and bring to a boil, stirring all the time. Simmer for one minute and serve the fish with the sauce spooned over.

CHINA

SHRIMP AND GINGER ROLLS

SERVES 4 • PREPARATION: 20 MINUTES • COOKING: 6 MINUTES

12 raw jumbo shrimp,
   peeled and deveined
12 spring roll wrappers,
   roughly 7-in square, or
   in diameter
2 tsp fresh ginger puree
2 large garlic cloves, peeled
   and crushed
4 scallions, trimmed and
   chopped fine
1 egg white, lightly beaten
Peanut oil for deep-frying

These could be served as a hot appetizer with a small salad garnish or as a party nibble with a small bowl of sweet soy sauce as a dip. To prevent the spring roll wrappers uncurling as they fry, brush the edges with lightly forked egg white to ensure they stay firmly glued together.

1   Place a jumbo shrimp in the center of a spring roll wrapper. Spread with a little ginger puree and crushed garlic and top with a few pieces of scallion.

2   Brush the edges of the wrapper with egg white and fold up around the shrimp to make a neat parcel, tucking in the sides and pressing the edges together to seal.

3   Repeat with the remaining shrimp, wrappers, ginger, garlic, and scallions to make 12 rolls.

4   Heat the peanut oil to 350°F for deep-frying and fry the rolls four at a time for two minutes each, or until crisp and golden. Drain on a paper towel and serve hot.

CHINA

LEMON & GINGER SCALLOPS

SERVES 4 · PREPARATION: 15 MINUTES · COOKING: 10 MINUTES

Scallops:

3 tbsp peanut oil

$^1/_2$ red bell pepper, seeded and sliced

1 zucchini, sliced

4 scallions, trimmed and sliced

4 water chestnuts, sliced

2 oz frozen peas

1 lb queen (small) scallops

Lemon and ginger sauce:

1 tbsp cornstarch

$^1/_2$ cup freshly squeezed lemon juice

$1^1/_4$ cups chicken broth

2 tbsp clear honey

1 tbsp granulated brown sugar

1-in piece gingerroot, peeled and grated

The sharp citrus sauce is sweetened with honey and given an extra tang by the addition of fresh ginger grated fine. Shrimp can be used instead of the scallops if you prefer.

1   Heat 2 tablespoons oil in a wok and stir-fry the red bell pepper, zucchini, and scallions over a high heat for two minutes. Add the water chestnuts and frozen peas and stir-fry for a further two minutes. Remove from the wok and set aside.

2   Add the remaining peanut oil to the wok and when really hot, stir-fry the scallops in two batches for one to two minutes each until just cooked. Remove from the wok and set aside.

3   To make the sauce, whisk together the cornstarch and lemon juice until smooth. Pour into the wok and stir in the broth, honey, sugar, and ginger.

4   Stir over a low heat until the sauce comes to a boil. Lower the heat and simmer for one minute until it thickens and clears.

5   Return the vegetables and scallops to the wok and stir for 30 seconds until they are coated with the sauce and have heated through. Serve with fried rice.

CHINA

CRUNCHY SHRIMP & SALMON BALLS

SERVES 4 • PREPARATION: 15 MINUTES • COOKING: 20 MINUTES

9 oz raw shrimp, peeled
9 oz salmon fillet, skinned
and cut into chunks
2 scallions, chopped fine
$^1/_2$ tsp fresh ginger puree
1 small egg, beaten
4 thin slices of white bread,
crusts removed
Peanut oil for deep-frying

Slightly stale bread is easier to cut into small cubes because it is drier and firmer than fresh bread. If using fresh bread, cut the slices with kitchen scissors rather than a knife to prevent the crumb tearing. Dark soy sauce or sweet and sour sauce makes an excellent dip.

1   Preheat the oven to 350°F.

2   Mince or chop the shrimp and salmon finely. Place in a bowl and stir in the scallions, ginger, and egg.

3   Cut the bread slices into tiny cubes and spread them out on a baking sheet. Place in the oven for five minutes until the cubes are dry but not toasted.

4   Shape the shrimp mixture into 12 small balls and roll in the bread cubes until they are well coated.

5   Heat oil for deep-frying to 350°F and deep-fry the shrimp balls in batches for two to three minutes until golden brown. Drain on paper towels. Serve at once with a dipping sauce.

CHINA

PORK IN GINGERED HOI SIN SAUCE

SERVES 4 • PREPARATION: 15 MINUTES • COOKING: 15 MINUTES

4 tbsp peanut oil
1 lb lean pork, cut into thin strips
1 red onion, peeled and sliced fine
1 red bell pepper, seeded and chopped
1 tsp fresh ginger puree
2 garlic cloves, peeled and chopped
3 oz baby corn
6 tbsp hoi sin sauce
2 tbsp rice vinegar
2 tbsp light soy sauce

When slicing meat for stir-frying, cut across the grain of the meat so the fibers are short and the meat stays tender when cooked. It is also important to heat the oil until it sizzles before adding the meat so the pieces seal quickly and do not start to stew and toughen.

1   Heat half the peanut oil in a wok and stir-fry half the pork over a brisk heat for two to three minutes until the meat is sealed and starting to brown. Drain from the wok and stir-fry the rest of the pork, draining it from the wok when cooked.

2   Add the remaining peanut oil to the wok, lower the heat to medium, and stir-fry the onion for one minute. Add the red bell pepper and ginger and stir-fry for two minutes.

3   Add the garlic and baby corn and stir-fry for two minutes. Stir in the hoi sin sauce, rice vinegar, and light soy sauce and return all the pork to the wok.

4   Simmer for two minutes until all the ingredients are piping hot. Serve with boiled rice or egg noodles.

CHINA

GINGERED DUCK WITH PINEAPPLE & LYCHEES

SERVES 4 · MARINATING: 5 HOURS · PREPARATION: 20 MINUTES · COOKING: 10 MINUTES

Make sure the skillet is very hot before you add the duck so the flesh seals quickly and the skin becomes crisp. Because duck skin contains a lot of fat, it is not necessary to add extra to the pan for frying.

4 duck breasts
2 tsp grated gingerroot
$^1/_2$ tsp salt
1 tsp ground black pepper

Sauce:
$^3/_4$ cup chicken broth
2 tsp cornstarch
4 tbsp light soy sauce
1 tsp granulated sugar
4 tbsp rice wine
$^1/_2$ tsp sweet chili sauce
1 slice of pineapple, cut into small pieces
8 lychees, peeled, stoned, and halved
2 tbsp chopped cilantro leaf

1 Cut each duck breast into three or four pieces and place in a dish. Mix together the gingerroot, salt, and pepper, rub over the duck pieces, and leave in a cool place for several hours.

2 Heat a heavy non-stick skillet, add the duck, and dry-fry for five minutes until the skin of the duck is crisp and the flesh is cooked. Remove from the skillet and set aside.

3 Pour off the fat from the skillet and wipe it out with a paper towel.

4 To make the sauce, mix a little of the broth with the cornstarch until smooth, and pour into the skillet with the rest of the broth, light soy sauce, sugar, rice wine, and chili sauce.

5 Bring to a boil, stirring until thickened and smooth. Return the duck to the skillet and add the pineapple pieces and halved lychees. Simmer for one to two minutes and serve with cilantro scattered over. Serve with steamed or boiled rice.

1½ oz dried Chinese
   mushrooms
4 cups chicken broth
2 tbsp light soy sauce
2 tbsp rice wine
½ tsp fresh ginger puree
½ tsp sesame oil
1 head of bok choy,
   shredded fine
16 won tons
4 scallions, trimmed
   and sliced thin

CHINA

WON TON SOUP

SERVES 4 • PREPARATION: 15 MINUTES (PLUS SOAKING) • COOKING: 25 MINUTES

Packs of fresh or frozen ready-made won tons filled with a meat, shrimp, or vegetable stuffing are available from Asian food stores. Thaw frozen won tons thoroughly before adding to the soup but spread them out on a plate while they are defrosting or the wrappers will stick together and tear when you try and separate them.

1   Put the dried mushrooms in a bowl, pour over boiling water to cover, and leave to soak for 30 minutes until tender.

2   Drain the mushrooms and cut into quarters if large. Strain the soaking liquid through a fine sieve into a measuring jug to remove any grit.

3   In a large saucepan, bring the broth to a boil. Add the light soy sauce, rice wine, ginger, and sesame oil and simmer for five minutes. Add ¾ cup soaking liquid, Chinese mushrooms, and bok choy and simmer gently for 10 minutes.

4   Meanwhile, bring a large saucepan of water to a boil, drop in the won tons one by one, and simmer for five minutes or according to the package instructions. Lift out the won tons with a draining spoon and add to the soup.

5   Spoon the soup into bowls and serve with the scallions scattered over.

CHINA

SALMON MARINATED IN GINGERED TEA

SERVES 4 • MARINATING: 3–4 HOURS
PREPARATION: 10 MINUTES (PLUS STANDING & COOLING) • COOKING: 10 MINUTES

1 Chinese black tea bag
³/₄ cup boiling water
1-in piece of gingerroot,
    peeled and chopped fine
3 tbsp dark soy sauce
¹/₂ tsp freshly ground
    Szechuan pepper
1 tbsp clear honey
Four 5-oz salmon fillets
2 tbsp peanut oil

Tea is a favorite drink in China, and in this recipe it is used to add fragrance to the spicy marinade for the salmon. Black tea has a stronger flavor than green, so look for varieties such as Keemun or Lapsang Souchong. Serve the salmon with stir-fried or steamed green vegetables and boiled rice.

1   Place the tea bag in a heatproof measuring jug and pour over the boiling water. Leave to stand for five minutes, then remove the tea bag and stir in the ginger, dark soy sauce, pepper, and honey. Leave until cold.

2   Place the salmon fillets side by side in a shallow dish and pour over the tea mixture. Cover and leave in a cool place to marinate for three to four hours, turning over the salmon fillets occasionally.

3   Lift the fillets out of the marinade, letting the excess drain off them. Heat the peanut oil in a large non-stick skillet, add the salmon skin side down, and fry over a brisk heat for two minutes. Turn the fillets over, lower the heat to medium, and cook for a further three minutes or until the salmon is done.

4   Remove the salmon from the skillet and keep warm. Pour the marinade left in the dish into the skillet and boil for two to three minutes until reduced by half. Spoon the reduced marinade over the salmon and serve at once.

CAULIFLOWER & BELL PEPPER TEMPURA WITH GINGER DIPPING SAUCE

SERVES 4–6 • PREPARATION: 15 MINUTES (PLUS STANDING) • COOKING: 15 MINUTES

Dipping sauce:
6 tbsp Japanese soy sauce
2 tbsp rice vinegar
Small knob of gingerroot, peeled and chopped fine
$^1/_2$ tsp sweet chili sauce

Batter:
2 egg yolks
1$^1/_4$ cups chilled water
1$^3/_4$ cups all-purpose flour
$^1/_2$ tsp ground ginger

Tempura:
1 cauliflower, divided into small florets
Peanut oil for deep-frying
1 red bell pepper, seeded and cut into 8 wedges
1 orange bell pepper, seeded and cut into 8 wedges

Most batters benefit from being left to stand for an hour before using so that the gluten in the flour has time to develop and give a lighter result. As tempura batter is very light already, it can be made and used immediately.

1 To make the dipping sauce, stir the ingredients together and pour into a small serving bowl. Leave to stand for one to two hours to give the flavors time to develop.

2 To make the batter, whisk the egg yolks and water together in a bowl, beating until frothy. Sift in the flour and ginger and whisk until the dry ingredients are just mixed in. The batter should have the consistency of light cream so add a little more water if it is too thick.

3 To prepare the tempura, blanch the cauliflower florets in a pan of boiling water for two minutes or until almost tender. Drain.

4 Heat the peanut oil to 375°F for deep-frying. Using chopsticks or tongs, dip the florets and orange bell pepper wedges into the batter one at a time and fry in batches of six to eight pieces for three to four minutes until golden and crisp.

5 Drain the vegetables on a paper towel and serve hot with the dipping sauce.

¹/₂ cantaloupe melon
¹/₂ ogen melon
Large wedge of watermelon
1¹/₄ cups water
**2 tbsp granulated
    brown sugar**
4 tbsp rice wine
**2 pieces of preserved
    ginger, shredded**

CHINA

CHILLED MELON IN GINGER SYRUP

SERVES 4 • PREPARATION: 15 MINUTES (PLUS COOLING & CHILLING) • COOKING: 1 MINUTE

A refreshing summer dessert that can be made with any selection of melons you have available, but include watermelon if you can, as its deep red flesh provides a striking contrast to pale-colored fruit.

1 Peel the cantaloupe and ogen melons, discard the seeds, and cut the flesh into bite-size pieces. Cut the unpeeled watermelon into small wedges. Place in a serving bowl.

2 Put the water in a pan, add the sugar, and heat gently until dissolved. Simmer for one minute, remove from the heat, and stir in the rice wine and ginger. Leave to cool.

3 Pour the syrup over the melon and chill for one to two hours before serving.

THAILAND

THAI CRAB CAKES

MAKES 20 • PREPARATION: 30 MINUTES (PLUS CHILLING) • COOKING: 15 MINUTES

1 lb white crab meat, flaked
**4 oz snow peas, trimmed
    and chopped fine**
1¹/₂ tsp fresh ginger puree
Finely grated zest of 1 lime
1 tbsp Thai fish sauce
1 tbsp chives, chopped fine
1 egg white, lightly beaten
All-purpose flour, to dust
Peanut oil for deep-frying

Serve these as a light lunch or supper dish, or as a starter to a more formal meal. They also make an unusual snack, served on a platter with a sweet chili dip to accompany pre-dinner drinks.

1 Place the crab meat, snow peas, ginger puree, lime zest, fish sauce, and chives in a bowl and stir until evenly mixed.

2 Add the egg white and stir to bind the ingredients together.

3 With floured hands, shape the mixture into 20 small balls, flattening them into round cakes. Place on a plate or board, slightly spaced apart, and chill for one hour to firm up.

4 Heat the peanut oil to 325°F for deep-frying. Dust the crab cakes with flour and deep-fry in batches for about three minutes or until golden. Drain on a plate lined with absorbent paper towels and serve warm with a salad garnish or a spicy dipping sauce.

RIGHT Chilled melon in ginger syrup

CHILI

Chilies traveled from Central and South America to Asia via Africa and India. Dozens of different varieties exist but, as a general rule, the smaller the chili the hotter it will be. The heat comes not from the chili flesh but from the seeds and membranes inside, so if you want to reduce their fire, cut these out before adding the chili to a dish. Red chilies are ripened green chilies but although they have a slightly different flavor they can be equally fiery. A rich source of vitamins A and C, chilies can be bought fresh or dried and as a paste, powder, or sauce.

SHRIMP GREEN CURRY WITH BASIL

SERVES 4 • PREPARATION: 30 MINUTES • COOKING: 5–6 MINUTES

Curry paste:

6 medium green chilis, seeded and roughly chopped

2 stalks of lemon grass, outer leaves removed, chopped

2 tbsp roughly chopped cilantro leaves

2 tbsp roughly chopped Thai basil leaves

1 shallot, peeled and chopped

3 garlic cloves, peeled and roughly chopped

1 tsp shrimp paste

2 tsp ginger puree

4 kaffir lime leaves, chopped

Curry:

2 tbsp peanut oil

3 red shallots, peeled and sliced

7 oz pumpkin or butternut squash, peeled, seeded, and cut into small pieces

1 zucchini, sliced

1 tbsp fish sauce

1 tbsp granulated brown sugar

1³/₄ cups coconut milk

1 lb raw peeled shrimp

To garnish:

2 scallions, shredded

1 green chili, seeded and sliced fine

Thai basil leaves

Thai basil, known as *bai jorapa*, sweet basil, or holy basil, has an aniseed flavor quite different from the aromatic Italian or Greek basil. Bunches of it can be found in Chinese and Thai food stores.

1   To make the paste, blend all the ingredients in a food processor.

2   To make the curry, heat the peanut oil in a large skillet, add the shallot and pumpkin or butternut squash, and fry for five minutes, stirring occasionally.

3   Add the zucchini and 2 tablespoons of the curry paste and fry for a further two minutes. Any leftover curry paste can be stored in a small screw-top jar in the refrigerator.

4   Stir in the fish sauce, granulated sugar, and coconut milk. Bring to a boil, lower the heat, and simmer for 15 minutes until the pumpkin or butternut squash is tender.

5   Add the shrimp and simmer for two to three minutes until they turn pink. Serve garnished with the scallions, green chili, and Thai basil leaves.

CHINA

STIR-FRIED PORK WITH CHILI & PEANUTS

SERVES 4 • PREPARATION: 15 MINUTES • COOKING: 15 MINUTES

Only fry the peanuts until they are light golden as they will become darker once they have been removed from the wok. If fried until a deep brown the nuts will develop a bitter, unpleasant taste.

1   Whisk together the hoi sin sauce, dark soy sauce, and sweet chili sauce.

2   Heat 1 tablespoon of the peanut oil in a wok and stir-fry the peanuts for 15 to 20 seconds until golden. Drain from the wok and set to one side.

3   Add another tablespoon of peanut oil to the wok and stir-fry the pork in two or three batches over a high heat for three minutes until lightly browned. Remove from the wok and set aside.

4   Add the remaining peanut oil to the wok, lower the heat to medium, add the onion and stir-fry for three minutes. Add the orange bell pepper and mushrooms, stir-fry for two minutes, then add the red chili and bok choy and stir-fry for a further two to three minutes until the leaves of the bok choy start to wilt.

5   Return all the pork to the wok, pour in the chili sauce mix and toss together over the heat for one minute. Serve at once with the peanuts scattered over.

3 tbsp hoi sin sauce
2 tbsp dark soy sauce
2 tsp sweet chili sauce
3 tbsp peanut oil
2 oz unsalted peanuts
1 lb lean pork,
    cut into thin strips
1 large onion, peeled
    and sliced
1 orange bell pepper,
    seeded and sliced
4 oz shiitake or chestnut
    mushrooms, quartered
1 red chili, seeded
    and sliced fine
2 heads of bok choy,
    shredded

BARBECUED KOREAN LAMB WITH CUCUMBER PICKLE

SERVES 4 • MARINATING: 8 HOURS • PREPARATION: 15 MINUTES (PLUS STANDING)
COOKING: 5–6 MINUTES

Lamb:
2 tsp kochujang chili paste
2 tbsp rice vinegar
4 tbsp Japanese soy sauce
3 tbsp mirin
1 tsp sesame oil
12 lamb cutlets

Pickle:
1/2 cucumber, grated
1 tsp salt
3-in piece of white
   radish, grated
2 tsp sesame oil
2 tsp sesame seeds,
   lightly toasted

Kochujang is a Korean chili paste used for glazing meat or adding to stir-fries, stews, and dips. It can be bought from Asian stores but if you cannot find it, use whatever chili paste you have available.

1   Mix together the chili paste, rice vinegar, Japanese soy sauce, mirin, and sesame oil.

2   Lay the lamb cutlets in a single layer in a shallow dish and spoon the marinade over them. Cover and leave overnight in a cool place.

3   To make the pickle, place the grated cucumber in a colander set on a large plate to catch the drips, sprinkle with the salt and leave for 30 minutes.

4   Drain, rinse, and pat the cucumber dry with a paper towel. Mix with the grated radish.

5   Grill or barbecue the lamb cutlets for five to six minutes or until cooked to your liking, basting or brushing with any marinade left in the dish as they cook.

6   Serve the lamb with the cucumber pickle, with the sesame oil drizzled over and sprinkled with the sesame seeds.

THAI SHRIMP SKEWERS WITH COCONUT RICE

SERVES 4 • MARINATING: 1 HOUR • PREPARATION: 15 MINUTES • COOKING: 15 MINUTES

1½ lb raw tiger shrimp, peeled and deveined but tails left on
1 tsp fresh lemon grass puree
1 tsp fresh galangal puree
2 tsp mild chili paste
1 tbsp Thai fish sauce
1 oz creamed coconut
2½ cups vegetable broth
2 cups Thai fragrant rice
2 tbsp chopped fresh cilantro
1 green chili, seeded and chopped fine

Serve the skewers and rice with stir-fried snow peas with shiitake mushrooms (*see* page 142).

1 Thread the tiger shrimp onto skewers and place side-by-side in a shallow dish.

2 Mix together the lemon grass puree, galangal puree, chili paste, and Thai fish sauce and spread over the shrimp. Cover and leave to marinate for one hour.

3 Place the creamed coconut and vegetable broth in a large saucepan and heat gently until the coconut dissolves. Rinse the Thai fragrant rice in a colander under cold running water, then add to the saucepan of simmering broth.

4 Simmer for 10 to 12 minutes or until the rice is tender and has absorbed the stock.

5 While the rice is cooking, heat the grill to high. Line the grill rack with foil and place the shrimp skewers on it in a single layer. Grill for five minutes until the shrimp turn pink, turning the skewers over halfway.

6 Stir the cilantro and chopped green chili into the coconut rice, and serve with the shrimp skewers.

VEGETABLE FRITTERS WITH CHILI RELISH

SERVES 4–6 • PREPARATION: 30 MINUTES (PLUS SOAKING) • COOKING: 1½ HOURS

Chili relish:
½ oz large dried
   red chilis
Peanut oil for
   deep-frying
1 red bell pepper, seeded
   and chopped
4 red shallots, peeled
   and chopped
2 garlic cloves, peeled
   and chopped fine
½ cup chopped tomatoes
1 tsp shrimp paste
2 tbsp granulated
   brown sugar
4 fl oz fish sauce

Fritters:
8 snow peas,
   chopped fine
2 scallions, chopped fine
4 oz sweetcorn kernels
½ red bell pepper,
   chopped fine
1 tbsp crunchy peanut
   butter
1 tbsp fish sauce
1 tsp granulated sugar
1 tbsp chopped fresh mint
3 oz all-purpose flour
1 egg, beaten

To garnish:
Chopped scallions
Chili flowers

The quantities given for the relish will make more than is needed for the recipe but any leftover can be stored in a screw-top jar in the refrigerator for up to two weeks.

1   To make the chili relish, soak the red chilis in hot water for 30 minutes. Drain, cut open, and remove the seeds. Pat dry on paper towels.

2   Heat the peanut oil for deep-frying to 350°F and deep-fry the red chilis for two to three minutes until they are dark red. Drain on paper towels.

3   Transfer 2 tablespoons of the peanut oil to a wok and fry the red bell pepper and shallots for five minutes over a medium heat. Add the garlic, fry for two minutes and then stir in the tomatoes, red chilis, and shrimp paste.

4   Lower the heat and simmer gently for 30 minutes. Cool a little and then puree in a food processor with the sugar and fish sauce. Return the puree to the wok and cook very gently for about 40 minutes until dark, caramelized and thick, stirring frequently so it does not stick to the wok and burn.

5   To make the fritters, mix together the snow peas, scallions, sweetcorn, red bell pepper, crunchy peanut butter, fish sauce, sugar, and mint. Stir in the all-purpose flour and then the beaten egg to bind the mixture together.

6   Reheat the peanut oil for deep-frying to 350°F. Drop tablespoons of the mixture into the hot oil and fry for three to four minutes until golden brown. Drain and serve hot with a little of the chili relish. Garnish with chopped scallions and chili flowers.

THAILAND

THAI CHICKEN & NOODLE BROTH

SERVES 4 • PREPARATION: 15 MINUTES • COOKING: 20 MINUTES

2 tbsp peanut oil
1 red bell pepper, seeded
  and chopped fine
2 garlic cloves, peeled
  and crushed
2 small white eggplants,
  cut into wedges
2 oz pea eggplant, removed
  from their stalk
2 shiitake mushrooms,
  quartered
1 tbsp Thai red curry paste
2 tbsp tomato ketchup
3/4 cup coconut cream
3 boneless chicken breasts,
  cut into bite-size pieces
3 cups chicken broth
2 tbsp light soy sauce
Juice of 1 lime
1 tsp granulated
  brown sugar
6 oz dried medium egg
  noodles, broken into
  short lengths

To garnish:
1 red chili, shredded fine

Thai eggplant is very different from the large purple and black-skinned Mediterranean variety common in the West. This recipe uses two different types of Thai eggplant—the small round variety that has a pale green, almost white skin, and pea eggplants that grow in small clusters and have a sharp, slightly bitter flavor.

1   In a wok, heat the peanut oil and stir-fry the red bell pepper and garlic for three to four minutes over a medium heat until the pepper is almost tender.

2   Add the eggplant and shiitake mushrooms and cook for two minutes.

3   Add the Thai red curry paste and cook for 30 seconds. Stir in the tomato ketchup and coconut cream, cook for one minute, and then add the chicken, broth, light soy sauce, lime juice, and brown sugar.

4   Simmer for 10 minutes. Meanwhile, cook the egg noodles in a saucepan of boiling water for four minutes. Drain and divide between four serving bowls.

5   Spoon over the chicken broth and serve sprinkled with the shredded red chili.

Chili sauce:

4 oz large red chilis, seeded and chopped fine

3 garlic cloves, peeled and crushed

$^1/_2$ cup rice vinegar

5 oz superfine sugar

2 tbsp fish sauce

1 green chili, seeded and chopped

Squid:

1 lb squid, cleaned and cut into small pieces

3 tbsp cornstarch

$^1/_4$ tsp chili powder

Salt and freshly ground black pepper

Peanut oil for deep-frying

VIETNAM

CRISP PEPPERED SQUID WITH CHILI SAUCE

SERVES 4 • PREPARATION: 20 MINUTES (PLUS COOLING) • COOKING: 15 MINUTES

Heat the peanut oil to the correct temperature before adding the squid so it cooks quickly and does not become tough and tasteless. Score the flesh in a criss-cross pattern beforehand to help speed up the cooking process. If the squid has previously been frozen, thaw it completely and blot dry with paper towels because any remaining moisture will cause it to spit dangerously in the hot oil.

1 To make the sauce, put the red chilis, garlic, rice vinegar, and sugar in a saucepan and heat gently until the sugar dissolves. Simmer until the liquid reduces to a syrup. Stir in the fish sauce and green chilis and leave to cool.

2 To cook the squid, lightly score the pieces in a criss-cross pattern with a sharp knife. Season the cornstarch with the chili powder, a little salt, and plenty of freshly ground black pepper and use to dust the squid until it is evenly covered.

3 Heat the peanut oil for deep-frying to 350°F and fry the squid in two batches for about two minutes or until crisp. Drain on paper towels and serve with the sauce.

CHINA

PEARL RICE BALLS

MAKES 24 • PREPARATION: 25 MINUTES (PLUS SOAKING & DRYING) • COOKING: 20–25 MINUTES

6 oz short grain rice
8 oz minced pork
8 oz minced chicken
4 scallions, chopped fine
1 tsp fresh ginger puree
8 oz water chestnuts, chopped fine
1 tsp granulated sugar
3 tbsp dark soy sauce
1 tbsp tomato ketchup
1 red chili, deseeded and chopped very fine
3 tbsp chopped cilantro leaf
2 tbsp almonds, chopped fine
1 egg, beaten
Chicken broth

Short grain or sushi rice can be used for the recipe but soak it in a bowl of cold water for two hours before use to get rid of excess starch. Cook the rice balls in a bamboo or metal steamer adding chicken broth to the pan below for extra flavor.

1 Put the rice in a bowl, cover with cold water, and leave to soak for two hours. Drain the rice and spread out on a large plate to dry.

2 In a bowl, mix together the pork, chicken, scallions, ginger puree, water chestnuts, sugar, dark soy sauce, tomato ketchup, red chili, cilantro, and almonds. Stir in the beaten egg, mixing well.

3 With damp hands, form the mixture into 24 walnut-sized balls and roll in the rice to coat. Place the balls in a lightly greased steamer.

4 Bring a pan of chicken broth to a boil and steam the rice balls for 20 to 25 minutes or until the rice and meat are cooked.

CHINA

SHRIMP & CHILI OMELETS

SERVES 2 • PREPARATION: 15 MINUTES • COOKING: 10 MINUTES

2 tbsp peanut oil
4 oz baby button mushrooms, halved
5 oz beansprouts
2 tbsp light soy sauce
4 oz small peeled shrimp
4 large eggs
1/4 tsp ground Szechuan pepper
1 red chili, seeded and chopped very fine
1 tsp butter

Spoon the filling onto the omelet when the eggs are half set, and fold it over the filling when done. Alternatively, slide the omelet onto a plate and roll up.

1 Heat the peanut oil in a wok and stir-fry the mushrooms and beansprouts for three minutes. Add the light soy sauce and shrimp, stir-fry for one minute, then remove from the heat and set aside.

2 Beat together the eggs, Szechuan pepper, and red chili. Melt the butter in an 8-in non-stick skillet and pour in half the egg mixture. As the edges of the egg start to set, draw them toward the center of the wok with a fork, tilting the wok so the uncooked egg runs to the edge.

3 When the eggs have set underneath, spoon half the filling over one side of the omelet. When they are completely set, fold the omelet over the filling and turn onto a warmed serving plate. Cook a second omelet in the same way using the remaining eggs and filling.

VIETNAM

SEARED CHILI SCALLOPS

SERVES 4 • MARINATING: 15 MINUTES • PREPARATION: 20 MINUTES • COOKING: 5–7 MINUTES

12 scallops
3 tbsp peanut oil
1 tbsp sesame oil
Juice of 1 lime
2 tbsp light soy sauce
1 tsp clear honey
1 garlic clove, peeled
   and crushed
1 tsp chili sauce
2 carrots, sliced thin
1 red bell pepper, seeded
   and sliced thin
8 scallions, sliced
4 oz lotus root, peeled and
   sliced thin
1 green chili, seeded and
   chopped fine

Remove the roes from the scallops or leave them on as preferred. Scallops should be seared quickly over a high heat; if they are left to cook for too long, their delicate flesh will soon become tough.

1   Spread out the scallops in a shallow dish. Mix together 1 tablespoon peanut oil, the sesame oil, lime juice, light soy sauce, clear honey, garlic, and chili sauce and pour over the scallops. Set aside for 15 minutes.

2   Drain the scallops, reserving the marinade, and thread onto four skewers. Sear briefly in a heavy non-stick skillet or griddle for one to two minutes on each side until lightly browned.

3   Meanwhile, heat the remaining peanut oil in a wok and stir-fry the carrots, red bell pepper, scallions, and lotus root for three to four minutes until starting to soften. Pour the reserved marinade over the vegetables and add the green chili. Stir-fry for one minute.

4   Divide the vegetables between serving plates and rest a scallop skewer on top.

JAPAN

SPICY BARBECUED TUNA

SERVES 4 • MARINATING: 2–3 HOURS • PREPARATION: 10 MINUTES • COOKING: 7–10 MINUTES

Four fresh 6-oz tuna steaks
4 tbsp light soy sauce
2 tbsp rice vinegar
2 tsp chili sauce
1 tsp granulated
   brown sugar

Cooking time for the tuna will depend on the thickness of the steak and also how rare you like to eat it. Serve the tuna with an Asian salad of shredded vegetables tossed with a sunflower oil, light soy sauce, and lime juice vinaigrette.

1   Trim any skin from the tuna and place the steaks in a shallow dish.

2   Mix together the light soy sauce, rice vinegar, chili sauce, and brown sugar, stirring until the sugar dissolves. Pour over the fish and turn the steaks over so both sides are coated with the marinade.

3   Cover and leave in a cool place for two to three hours or until ready to cook.

4   Barbecue the tuna for 7 to 10 minutes or cook on a lightly greased ridged grill pan, turning the steaks over half way and brushing with excess marinade.

CHINA

STIR-FRIED CHICKEN & RICE WITH SWEET CHILI SAUCE

SERVES 2 • MARINATING: 4 HOURS • PREPARATION: 15 MINUTES • COOKING: 15 MINUTES

Leaving the chicken to stand for several hours helps it absorb the flavors of the marinade but if you are pressed for time, the chili sauce, garlic, and soy mix can just be poured into the wok when you add the rice and peas.

12-oz chicken breasts, cut
   into small pieces
1 tbsp sweet chili sauce
2 tbsp dark soy sauce
1 garlic clove, peeled
   and crushed
2 tbsp peanut oil
2 eggs, lightly beaten
3 scallions, chopped
1 celery stick, chopped
1 carrot, diced fine
12 oz cooked long-grain rice
2 oz frozen peas
1 red chili, seeded
   and sliced

1   Spread out the chicken in a dish. Mix together the chili sauce, dark soy sauce, and garlic and spoon over the chicken, stirring until the pieces are coated. Cover and leave in a cool place to marinate for 4 hours.

2   Heat 1 tablespoon of peanut oil in a wok and pour in the eggs. Tilt the wok so the eggs cook to make a thin omelet. Slide the cooked omelet out of the wok onto a board, allow to cool a little, then roll up and slice thin.

3   Add the remaining peanut oil to the wok and stir-fry the chopped scallions with the celery and carrot for three minutes over a medium heat. Remove the vegetables from the wok and set aside.

4   Increase the heat to high. Drain the chicken from the dish, add to the wok and stir-fry over a brisk heat for three minutes. Add the rice and frozen peas, return the vegetables to the wok, and pour in any marinade left in the dish.

5   Toss everything together over the heat for three to four minutes until piping hot. Serve topped with the omelet strips and the sliced chili.

FRESH LIME & LIME LEAVES

Limes grow prolifically all over Southeast Asia and come in many varieties, from the smooth-skinned medium-sized fruit we are familiar with in the West to tiny kalamansi fruit that are considered to have the best flavored juice. Kaffir lime trees produce knobbly rough-skinned fruit that have a thick layer of pith and hot, spicy juice. Their grated zest is added to food but it is their leaves that are most commonly seen in the West. They can be added whole to curries, soups, and rice dishes or as an ingredient but they must be sliced wafer-thin to make them edible. The leaves can be bought fresh or dried.

VIETNAMESE LIME & MINT CHICKEN

SERVES 4 • MARINATING: 30 MINUTES • PREPARATION: 25 MINUTES
COOKING: 20 MINUTES

Dried beanthread noodles are made from mung beans and are often added to soups as they require little cooking beyond a brief immersion in hot liquid. Also known as "'glass," "jelly," or "transparent" noodles, they are equally delicious served cold in salads.

2 limes
5 tbsp fish sauce
2 garlic cloves, peeled
    and crushed
2 tbsp granulated sugar
$^1/_2$ tsp freshly ground
    black pepper
8 boneless chicken thighs
    or 4 chicken breasts
2 tbsp peanut oil
7 oz beanthread or
    vermicelli rice noodles
$^1/_2$ cucumber, cut into sticks
1 large carrot, cut into
    fine sticks
Small handful of
    mint sprigs

To garnish:
1 red chili, seeded and
    chopped fine
Lime zest

1   Peel the zest from one lime and cut into fine long shreds. Set aside. Squeeze the juice from both limes.

2   In a shallow dish, mix together the lime juice, fish sauce, garlic, sugar, and black pepper, stirring until the sugar dissolves. Add the chicken to the dish and baste with the marinade until well coated. Set aside for 30 minutes.

3   Heat the peanut oil in a large heavy skillet, add the chicken skin side down and cook for five minutes over a fairly high heat until the skin is browned. Lower the heat, turn the chicken breasts over, pour in any marinade left in the dish and cover the skillet. Cook for 10 minutes, then uncover the skillet and cook for a further five minutes or until the chicken is cooked through and caramelized.

4   Soak the noodles in a bowl of boiling water for three minutes or according to the package instructions. Drain and divide between serving dishes with the cucumber, carrot, and mint leaves.

5   Slice the chicken and arrange over the noodles. Garnish with the chopped red chili and the reserved lime zest.

THAILAND

CRAB, POMELO, & RICE NOODLE SALAD

SERVES 4 · PREPARATION: 15 MINUTES (PLUS COOLING)

As with green mangoes, green papayas are under-ripe fruit and they are a staple ingredient in Thai salads. Mixed with seafood, chopped chicken, or fried minced pork and sold freshly made by street vendors, the salads make a light but satisfying lunch for office and store workers.

9 oz medium rice noodles
Juice of 2 limes
1 red chili, seeded and
   sliced very thin
2 tbsp fish sauce
1 tsp granulated sugar
¹/₂ cucumber
1 pomelo
5 oz green papaya, peeled
   and grated
12 crab claws

To garnish:
Extra lime wedges

1 Cook the rice noodles according to the package instructions and drain.

2 Mix together the lime juice, red chili, fish sauce, and sugar, stirring until the sugar dissolves. Toss with the warm noodles and set them aside to cool.

3 Cut the cucumber into long strips using a vegetable peeler. Peel the pomelo, pull away the pith, and break the flesh into bite-size segments.

4 Add the cucumber, pomelo, grated green papaya, and crab claws to the noodles and toss lightly together.

5 Transfer to a serving dish and serve with extra lime wedges to squeeze over.

JAPAN

PAN-FRIED SCALLOPS WITH PONZU SAUCE

SERVES 4 • PREPARATION: 10 MINUTES • COOKING: 5 MINUTES

Ponzu or "pon-su" is a Japanese dressing or dipping sauce for grilled meat and seafood made by mixing equal quantities of soy sauce and freshly squeezed lime or lemon juice. *Dashi*—a seaweed-based stock of dried kelp and dried bonito flakes—is sometimes added as well.

Sauce:
4 tbsp freshly squeezed
   lime juice
4 tbsp Japanese soy sauce
2 lime slices

Scallops:
2 tbsp peanut oil
12 scallops
4 scallions, sliced
1 red shallot, peeled
   and sliced
4 oz beansprouts
1 carrot, cut into sticks
2 oz young spinach leaves,
   shredded

1   To make the sauce, mix the lime juice and Japanese soy sauce together. Add the lime slices and set aside until needed.

2   To cook the scallops, heat one tablespoon of peanut oil in a heavy skillet and sear the scallops for one minute on each side or until just cooked. Remove from the skillet.

3   Add the rest of the peanut oil to the skillet with the scallions, shallot, beansprouts, carrot, and spinach and stir-fry for one to two minutes until the vegetables have started to soften.

4   Divide the vegetables between serving dishes, top with the scallops, and pour over the sauce.

THAILAND

LIME-MARINATED PORK SKEWERS

SERVES 4 • MARINATING: 1–2 HOURS • PREPARATION: 20 MINUTES • COOKING: 5 MINUTES

Chicken could be substituted for the pork if you prefer. When slicing the lime leaf to make the dipping sauce, use small sharp scissors or a scalpal—if the slices are not wafer thin they will be unpleasant to eat.

Dipping sauce:
3 tbsp light soy sauce
1 kaffir lime leaf, sliced
   very fine
1 tbsp fish sauce
Juice of 1 lime
1 tsp granulated
   brown sugar
1 green chili, seeded
   and sliced fine

Skewers:
3 large garlic cloves, peeled
   and crushed
Juice of 3 limes
1 tbsp granulated
   brown sugar
1 tbsp fish sauce
1 tbsp light soy sauce
1 tsp fresh lemon grass
   puree
$^{1}/_{2}$ tsp fresh ginger puree
1 lb lean pork steaks, cut
   into 1-in cubes

1   To make the dipping sauce, stir the ingredients together until the sugar dissolves. Set aside for at least one hour to allow the flavors to develop.

2   Meanwhile, prepare the skewers, mix the garlic, lime juice, brown sugar, fish sauce, light soy sauce, lemon grass puree, and ginger puree together in a bowl, stirring until the sugar dissolves.

3   Add the pork and stir so the cubes are well coated. Cover and leave in a cool place to marinate for one to two hours.

4   Drain the pork and thread the cubes onto skewers. Grill or barbecue for five minutes, turning the skewers over once or twice and brushing with any marinade left in the bowl.

5   Serve the skewers hot with the dipping sauce.

CHINA

HOT & SOUR SHRIMP & TOFU SOUP

SERVES 4 · PREPARATION: 15 MINUTES · COOKING: 20 MINUTES

3/4 oz dried Chinese black
   mushrooms
4 cups chicken broth
7 oz raw tiger shrimp
4 slices of root ginger
7 oz firm tofu, cut into
   small cubes
4 scallions, cut into
   thin strips
2 small dried chilis, seeded
   and chopped fine
2 tbsp fish sauce
2 tbsp lime juice
4 lime leaves

Chinese black mushrooms are available dried in bags from Chinese supermarkets and must be soaked in warm water before cooking so they rehydrate and swell. The soaking liquid makes an excellent vegetable broth but before adding it to a dish, strain it first to get rid of any grit that was trapped in the mushrooms.

1 Soak the Chinese black mushrooms in warm water for 20 minutes. Drain and cut into bite-size pieces.

2 Put the chicken broth in a saucepan. Peel the tiger shrimp and add the shells to the broth with the ginger. Bring to a boil and simmer for 10 minutes. Strain the broth, discarding the shells and ginger.

3 Bring the broth back to a boil, add the Chinese black mushrooms, tofu, scallions, chilis, fish sauce, lime juice, and lime leaves and simmer for five minutes.

4 Devein the shrimp and add them to the soup. Stir well and cook for two minutes or until the shrimp turn pink.

VIETNAM

CRISP-FRIED SQUID RINGS WITH LIME & CHILI SAUCE

SERVES 2 • MARINATING: 5 HOURS • PREPARATION: 20 MINUTES • COOKING: 10 MINUTES

Sauce:
1 large garlic clove, peeled and crushed
1 red chili, seeded and chopped fine
2 tsp granulated brown sugar
Juice of 1 lime
3 tbsp light soy sauce
1 tbsp Thai or Vietnamese fish sauce
2 tbsp water

Squid:
1 lb squid, cleaned and cut into rings
1 large garlic clove, peeled and crushed
3 tbsp peanut oil, plus extra for deep-frying
3 tbsp lime juice
1 red chili, seeded and chopped fine
8 oz all-purpose flour, plus extra to dust
1/4 cup light beer
1 egg white

Marinating the squid rings before cooking not only helps tenderize them but allows them to absorb the flavors of the marinade.

1   To make the sauce, mix together all the ingredients, stirring until the sugar dissolves. Pour into a small bowl and set aside for several hours to give the flavors time to develop.

2   Meanwhile, put the squid rings in a bowl. Mix together the garlic, 3 tablespoons peanut oil, lime juice, and red chili and pour over the squid. Stir until the rings are well coated, then cover and leave in a cool place to marinate for four hours.

3   Sift 8 oz all-purpose flour into a bowl, make a well in the center and pour in half the light beer. Whisk this into the flour and then gradually whisk in the rest of the beer until you have a smooth batter. Leave to stand for one hour or longer.

4   Just before you are ready to cook the squid, whisk the egg white until standing in soft peaks and fold into the batter.

5   Drain the squid rings and dust lightly with all-purpose flour. Heat the peanut oil for deep-frying to 350°F, coat the squid in the batter, and deep-fry in batches for about two minutes each or until golden and crisp. Drain on paper towels.

6   Serve the squid rings with the chili sauce for dipping or spooning over.

CHICKEN, BROCCOLI, & TOFU STIR-FRY

SERVES 4 • MARINATING: 2–3 HOURS • PREPARATION: 15 MINUTES • COOKING: 15 MINUTES

9 oz firm tofu, cut into ¹/₂-in cubes
2 chicken breasts, skinned, boned, and cut into bite-size pieces
3 tbsp dark soy sauce
Juice of 1 lime
2 tbsp oyster sauce
1 tsp clear honey
3 tbsp peanut oil
3 oz cashews
1 large carrot, cut into sticks
6 oz Chinese broccoli florets
6 scallions, sliced

Tofu is made from soya milk using a process similar to making cheese. A true "superfood," it is rich in vegetable protein, contains all eight essential amino acids, is cholesterol-free, low in saturated fats and carbohydrates, and an excellent source of calcium.

1   Spread out the tofu and chicken in a shallow dish. Mix together the dark soy sauce, lime juice, oyster sauce, and clear honey with 1 tablespoon of the peanut oil and spoon over the tofu and chicken, turning the pieces over until well coated. Cover the dish and leave to marinate in a cool place for two to three hours.

2   Heat 1 tablespoon of peanut oil in a wok, add the cashews, and stir-fry for about 30 seconds until golden. Drain from the wok and set aside.

3   Add the carrot and Chinese broccoli to the wok and stir-fry over a medium heat for four to five minutes. Add the scallions and stir-fry for a further two minutes or until the carrot and broccoli are almost tender. Remove the vegetables and set aside.

4   Heat the remaining peanut oil in the wok. Lift the tofu and chicken from the marinade and add to the wok. Stir-fry over a high heat for three to four minutes, then return the vegetables to the wok and pour in any marinade remaining in the dish.

5   Toss all the ingredients together for two minutes until piping hot. Scatter over the cashews and serve at once with noodles.

THAILAND

LIME-DRESSED SHRIMP SALAD

SERVES 4 • PREPARATION: 15 MINUTES (PLUS COOLING) • COOKING: 1–2 MINUTES

Choose green, unripe mangoes for this salad because ripe, golden-fleshed ones will be too sweet and have too soft a texture.

1 For the dressing, whisk the ingredients together until the sugar dissolves. Set aside.

2 To make the salad, heat the sunflower oil in a wok and stir-fry the tiger shrimp for one to two minutes until they turn pink. Transfer to a bowl and pour over the dressing, stirring so all the shrimp are coated. Leave to cool.

3 Arrange the salad leaves, mango, red bell pepper, and cucumber on a serving dish and spoon the shrimp and dressing on top.

4 Serve with lime wedges to squeeze over and Lotus Chips (*see* page 126).

Dressing:
5 tbsp sunflower oil
Juice of 2 limes
2 tbsp light soy sauce
$^1/_2$ tsp superfine sugar

Salad:
1 tbsp sunflower oil
1 lb 2 oz raw tiger shrimp, peeled
4 oz mixed salad leaves (oriental or red stalk leaves)
1 green mango, peeled and flesh cut into fine sticks
$^1/_2$ red bell pepper, seeded and cut into fine sticks
2 oz cucumber, cut into fine sticks

To garnish:
Lime wedges
Lotus Chips

THAILAND

GRILLED SWORDFISH WITH LIME & CILANTRO

SERVES 2 • MARINATING: 1–2 HOURS • PREPARATION: 5 MINUTES • COOKING: 10 MINUTES

Four 6-oz swordfish steaks
1 tbsp peanut oil
1 tbsp Thai fish sauce
2 tbsp dark soy sauce
2 tsp granulated brown
sugar
2 tbsp freshly squeezed
lime juice
2 tbsp chopped fresh
cilantro leaf
1 red chili, seeded and sliced
very fine
3 oz fresh spinach leaves

To garnish:
Extra lime wedges to
squeeze over

Fish and citrus fruits make natural partners, and fresh lime goes particularly well with an oily, firm-fleshed fish like swordfish. Accompany with a mixed salad or a green vegetable such as spinach, as in this recipe.

1   Place the swordfish steaks side by side in a shallow dish. Mix the peanut oil, fish sauce, dark soy sauce, brown sugar, lime juice, cilantro leaf, and red chili together, and pour over the fish.

2   Cover and leave to marinate in a cool place for one to two hours.

3   Lift the fish from the marinade, place on a grill rack or in a hot ridged grill pan and cook for two to three minutes on each side, depending on the thickness of the steaks, until just cooked through.

4   Meanwhile, pour the marinade left in the dish into a wok and bubble until reduced by half. Add the spinach leaves and simmer until they are wilted.

5   Spoon the spinach onto serving plates, place the swordfish steaks on top, and spoon over any juices left in the wok. Serve with extra lime wedges.

LIME LECHE FLAN

SERVES 6 • PREPARATION: 15 MINUTES (PLUS COOLING) • COOKING: 50-55 MINUTES

¹/₂ cup granulated sugar
²/₃ cup water
3 large eggs
2 large egg yolks
¹/₃ cup superfine sugar
3 cups canned evaporated milk or ordinary full fat milk
Zest and juice of 1 lime, grated fine

Filipinos have incorporated many Spanish dishes into their native cuisine, including the popular caramel custard known as "flan." This variation is flavored with finely shredded lime zest and juice which provides a pleasing foil to the sweet caramel and creamy custard.

1 Preheat the oven to 325°F.

2 Warm the granulated sugar and water in a small heavy-based saucepan over a low heat until the sugar dissolves. Bring the syrup to a boil and keep boiling until it turns golden brown—don't let it get too dark or the caramel will have a bitter taste.

3 Pour the caramel into six ramekins or other small heatproof dishes, tilting them so the caramel coats the bases and comes halfway up the sides.

4 Whisk the whole eggs and yolks together in a bowl and then whisk in the superfine sugar. Pour the milk into a saucepan and heat it gently until bubbles form on the surface.

5 Pour the hot milk onto the whisked egg mixture, whisking constantly so it is evenly incorporated. Strain the custard into a large jug and stir in the lime zest and juice.

6 Pour the custard into the ramekins and stand them in a roasting pan filled with enough warm, but not boiling, water to come halfway up the sides of the dishes. Bake in the oven for 40 to 45 minutes or until just set.

7 Remove the ramekins from the pan and leave the custards to cool before turning out onto serving dishes.

WATERMELON & LIME ICE

SERVES 6–8 · PREPARATION: 10 MINUTES (PLUS COOLING AND FREEZING)

1¹/₄ cups sparkling mineral water
6 oz superfine sugar
²/₃ cup watermelon juice
¹/₃ cup freshly squeezed lime juice

To garnish:
Lime wedges

A refreshing palate cleanser to serve between courses or the perfect cool-down after a fiery or spicy meal. If you want to give the ice an extra kick, spoon over a little sake, vodka, gin, or other clear spirit just before serving.

1   Warm the sparkling mineral water and sugar in a saucepan over a low heat until the sugar dissolves. Bring to a boil, then remove from the heat and set aside.

2   Stir the sugar syrup into the watermelon juice with the lime juice. Pour into a shallow freezer container or tray and freeze for about four hours until the ice is firm enough to be mashed with a fork but not frozen solid.

3   Spoon into chilled glasses and serve with a lime wedge on the side of each glass.

THAILAND

TROPICAL FRUIT SALAD WITH LIME & PAPAYA SAUCE

SERVES 4 · PREPARATION: 20 MINUTES

Fruit salad:
1¹/₂ lb tropical fruits (prepared weight) such as mango, pineapple, rambutan, longan

Sauce:
1 ripe medium-size papaya, peeled and seeded
Zest and juice of 2 limes, grated fine
About ²/₃ cup tropical fruit juice
Kaffir lime leaves, to decorate

Seductively aromatic when ripe, papayas are highly prized in Asian countries, not just for their flavor but also their healing properties. An open wound is said to heal more quickly after the application of a papaya poultice.

1   Prepare the fruit as necessary and cut into bite-size pieces.

2   To make the sauce, roughly chop the papaya flesh and place in a food processor with three-quarters of the lime zest and all the juice. Add the tropical fruit juice and reduce to a smooth puree, adjusting the amount of juice, if necessary, according to the size of the papaya.

3   Serve the sauce with the fruit salad and the remaining lime zest scattered over. Decorate each serving with a lime leaf.

LEFT   Tropical fruit salad with lime & papaya sauce

SOY

As well as the ubiquitous soy sauce, soy beans are made into a variety of stir-fry and cooking sauces. Styles of soy sauce vary from country to country, a good all-purpose brand being shoyu, a naturally brewed Japanese soy sauce which is medium strength and will not overwhelm other ingredients.

Tamari is another soy sauce from Japan that is strong, thick, and black with a distinctive flavor, while Indonesian *kecap manis* (manis meaning "sweet") is thick, black, with a syrup-like texture. Other sauces made from soy beans include black bean (made from salted, fermented black soy beans) and yellow bean (from yellow soy beans), both of which are popular in stir-fries, and hoi sin, a thick sweet barbecue sauce for brushing over meat or adding to dipping sauces and stir-fries.

CHINA

PORK & BELL PEPPERS IN BLACK BEAN SAUCE

SERVES 4 • PREPARATION: 15 MINUTES • COOKING: 7–8 MINUTES

Black beans are fermented, salted soy beans. Mixed with soy sauce and spices, they make a popular stir-fry sauce in China.

1 lb pork tenderloin
2 tbsp peanut oil
2 oz blanched almonds
1 red onion, peeled
 and sliced
1 carrot, cut into sticks
¹/₂ red bell pepper,
 seeded and sliced
¹/₂ yellow bell pepper,
 seeded and sliced
¹/₂ green bell pepper,
 seeded and sliced
³/₄ cup black bean
 stir-fry sauce

1 Cut the pork into thin strips across the grain of the meat.

2 Heat 1 tablespoon peanut oil in a wok and stir-fry the almonds for about 30 seconds until golden. Drain from the wok and set aside.

3 Add the remaining peanut oil to the wok and stir-fry the pork in two batches over a high heat for one to two minutes until browned. Remove from the wok and set aside.

4 Add a little more peanut oil to the wok if necessary and stir-fry the onion and carrot for one minute over a medium heat. Add the bell peppers and stir-fry for three minutes. Remove from the wok and set aside.

5 Pour the sauce into the pan, add the pork, and stir until the meat is coated. Return the vegetables to the wok and toss everything together for one minute or until piping hot.

CHINA

SIZZLING STEAK WITH BARBECUE SAUCE

SERVES 4 • PREPARATION 15 MINUTES • COOKING: 10 MINUTES

5 oz dried fine rice noodles
or 9 oz fresh noodles
4 tbsp hoi sin sauce
1 tbsp rice vinegar
1 tbsp light soy sauce
2 tbsp peanut oil
6 shallots, peeled and sliced
5 oz tenderstem broccoli
florets
1 red bell pepper, seeded
and chopped
4 oz baby corn, cut into
short lengths
12 oz rump or sirloin steak,
trimmed of fat and cut
into thin strips

Once the vegetables have been stir-fried, turn up the heat and get the wok really hot before you add the steak. It should be sealed quickly so it stays beautifully tender.

1   If using dried noodles, soak them according to the package instructions.

2   Whisk together the hoi sin sauce, rice vinegar, and light soy sauce.

3   Heat 1 tablespoon peanut oil in a wok and stir-fry the shallots, broccoli, and red bell pepper over a medium heat for three minutes. Add the baby corn and stir-fry for a further three minutes. Remove the vegetables and set aside.

4   Turn up the heat to high, add the remaining peanut oil, and stir-fry the steak for two minutes. Pour in the hoi sin mixture, add the noodles and broccoli, and return the vegetables to the wok.

5   Toss everything together for two to three minutes until piping hot, and serve immediately.

CANTONESE CHICKEN WITH SWEET & SOUR SAUCE

SERVES 4 • PREPARATION: 20 MINUTES • COOKING: 15 MINUTES

Sauce:
$^1/_2$ cup chicken broth
3 tbsp light soy sauce
$^1/_2$ tsp fresh ginger puree
1 tbsp clear honey
3 tbsp rice vinegar
2 tbsp tomato ketchup
1 tsp cornstarch

Chicken:
3 chicken breasts, cut into 1-in pieces
2 tbsp all-purpose flour
$^1/_2$ tsp mild chili powder
4 tbsp peanut oil
1 red onion, peeled and sliced
1 green bell pepper, seeded and chopped
$^1/_2$ red bell pepper, seeded and chopped

If you prefer a spicier dish, use a hotter chili powder, or increase the quantity to one teaspoon.

1 To make the sauce, place all the ingredients in a saucepan, except the cornstarch, and heat gently until the honey melts. Mix the cornstarch with 1 tablespoon cold water, stir into the pan and bring to a boil, stirring continuously until thickened and smooth.

2 Simmer the sauce for one minute, then remove from the heat and set aside.

3 Meanwhile, dust the chicken with the flour and chili powder. Heat 3 tablespoons peanut oil in a wok and stir-fry the chicken over a high heat in two batches for three to four minutes. Remove from the wok and set aside.

4 Add the remaining peanut oil to the wok, lower the heat to medium, and stir-fry the onion for two minutes. Add the bell peppers and stir-fry for three minutes.

5 Return all the chicken to the wok and pour in the sauce. Toss until the chicken and vegetables are coated, and simmer for one minute.

6 Serve at once with stir-fried or steamed rice.

CHINA

RED BRAISED SHRIMP

SERVES 4 · PREPARATION: 10 MINUTES · COOKING: 5 MINUTES

"Red cooking" is a traditional way of serving whole fish such as freshwater carp in China, but it works well with thick fillets of white fish or jumbo shrimp.

Prawns:
¹/₂ tsp fresh ginger puree
1 tbsp light soy sauce
1 tbsp rice wine
1 tsp sweet chili sauce
4 tbsp yellow bean sauce
¹/₂ cup fish broth
1 tsp granulated brown
    sugar
2 tbsp peanut oil
1 lb 2 oz large raw shrimp,
    peeled and deveined
Few drops of sesame oil
2 tbsp snipped chives

1   Mix together the ginger, light soy sauce, rice wine, chili sauce, yellow bean sauce, fish stock, and brown sugar, stirring until the sugar dissolves.

2   Heat the peanut oil in a wok, add the shrimp, and stir-fry for one minute. Remove the shrimp and sprinkle them with the sesame oil.

3   Add the sauce, bring to a simmer, and return the shrimp to the wok. Baste them with the sauce and braise gently for two to three minutes. Serve with the snipped chives sprinkled over.

4   Accompany the shrimp with egg noodles and stir-fried green vegetables such as snow peas, bell peppers, and zucchini.

JAPAN

PORK AND MANGO IN TERIYAKI SAUCE

SERVES 2 • MARINATING: 3–4 HOURS • PREPARATION: 15 MINUTES
COOKING: 10 MINUTES

12 oz lean pork, cut into thin strips
4 tbsp peanut oil
3 tbsp teriyaki sauce
1 tsp clear honey
$^1/_2$ tsp chili sauce
2 shallots, peeled and sliced
1 zucchini, chopped
4 oz button mushrooms, quartered
1 red bell pepper, seeded and chopped
1 small mango, peeled and flesh sliced

Bottles of teriyaki sauce are available from larger supermarkets or Asian food stores. If you cannot find it, substitute dark soy sauce instead.

1   Put the pork in a bowl. Mix together 2 tablespoons peanut oil, the teriyaki sauce, honey, and chili sauce and pour over the pork, tossing until the strips are coated. Cover and leave in a cool place to marinate for three to four hours.

2   Heat the remaining peanut oil in a wok and stir-fry the shallots over a medium heat for one minute. Add the zucchini, mushrooms, and bell pepper and stir-fry for three to four minutes until the vegetables start to soften. Remove from the wok and set aside.

3   Drain the pork from the marinade, add to the wok, and stir-fry over a high heat for two minutes. Add the mango and stir-fry for a further one minute.

4   Return the vegetables to the wok with any marinade left in the bowl and toss everything together over the heat for two minutes. Serve at once with egg noodles.

JAPAN

YAKITORI CHICKEN STICKS

SERVES 4 • MARINATING: 1–2 HOURS • PREPARATION: 10 MINUTES
COOKING: 6–8 MINUTES

1/2 cup Japanese
   soy sauce (shoyu)
4 tbsp mirin
2 tbsp sake
2 tbsp peanut oil
1/2 tsp fresh ginger puree
2 tbsp granulated
   brown sugar
Freshly ground black
   pepper
4 boneless chicken breasts
   or 8 thighs, skinned
1 green bell pepper, seeded
   and cut into small chunks

Fast food, Tokyo-style. These chicken skewers marinated in a sweet soy glaze and sold at round-the-clock snack bars and street food stalls make a popular snack for the city's workers.

1 Whisk together the soy sauce, mirin, sake, peanut oil, ginger puree, and sugar until the sugar dissolves. Season with freshly ground black pepper.

2 Cut the chicken into bite-size pieces and spread out in a shallow dish. Pour over the soy mixture, turning the chicken pieces over so they are well coated, cover, and leave in a cool place to marinate for one to two hours.

3 Thread the chicken pieces onto skewers with the green bell pepper chunks. Pour the marinade left in the dish into a small pan and boil until it reduces by half.

4 Grill the chicken skewers for three to four minutes on each side, basting with the reduced marinade as they cook.

HOI SIN DUCK WITH EGG FRIED RICE

SERVES 4 • MARINATING: 3–4 HOURS • PREPARATION: 15 MINUTES
COOKING: 20 MINUTES

Duck:
2 duck breasts
2 tbsp dark soy sauce
2 tbsp hoi sin sauce
1 tbsp lime juice
4 scallions
4 radishes
1 stick of celery

Egg fried rice:
2 tbsp peanut oil
4 oz mushrooms, sliced or chopped
2 eggs, beaten
8 oz long grain rice, cooked
2 oz frozen peas
4 oz small peeled shrimp

This is a great way to use up leftover cooked rice. Other vegetables can be used instead of the mushrooms and peas—diced carrots, bell peppers, beans, or zucchini would all be suitable.

1 For the duck, place the breasts in a shallow dish. Mix together the dark soy sauce, hoi sin sauce, and lime juice and spoon over. Cover and leave to marinate in a cool place for three to four hours.

2 Cut the scallions, radishes, and celery into very thin strips. Place in a bowl of water with a few ice cubes and leave in the refrigerator to curl while the duck is marinating.

3 For the rice, heat the peanut oil in a wok and fry the mushrooms over a medium heat for two minutes. Pour in the eggs, tilting the wok so they cover the base in a thin layer. As soon as the eggs start to set, scramble with a fork.

4 Add the rice, frozen peas, and shrimp and toss together for two or three minutes until hot. Transfer to a serving dish and keep warm.

5 Heat a heavy non-stick skillet until very hot. Lift the duck breasts from the dish, reserving the marinade, and add to the skillet skin side down. Sear until golden brown, turn over, and lower the heat. Cook the duck for a further five minutes or until done to your liking.

6 Remove the duck from the skillet and carve into thin slices. Tip any excess fat out of the skillet, add the reserved marinade, and bring to a boil.

7 Spoon the rice into individual bowls, arrange the duck slices on top and spoon over the skillet juices. Serve with the shredded vegetables.

CHINA

SHRIMP & PORK WON TONS

MAKES 20 • PREPARATION: 30 MINUTES • COOKING: 15 MINUTES

6 oz raw shrimp, peeled
 and deveined
3 water chestnuts,
 chopped fine
2 scallions, chopped fine
6 oz minced pork
1 tsp lemon grass puree
2 tbsp light soy sauce
1 tsp granulated sugar
2 tbsp fish sauce
1 tsp sesame oil
20 won ton wrappers
1 egg white, lightly beaten
Peanut oil for deep-frying

As you make the won tons, place them on a cutting board dusted with flour, a little way apart, so they don't stick to the board or each other.

1   Chop the shrimp fine and mix with the water chestnuts, scallions, pork, and lemon grass puree. Add the light soy sauce, sugar, fish sauce, and sesame oil, stirring until all the ingredients are well mixed.

2   Place a teaspoonful of the mixture in the center of a won ton wrapper, brush the edges of the wrapper with egg white, and gather up around the filling, squeezing the edges together at the top to form a "money-bag" shape. Make 20 won tons in the same way.

3   Heat the peanut oil for deep-frying to 325°F and fry the won tons in batches for three to four minutes until golden and crisp. Drain on paper towels and serve with a small bowl of soy, plum, or sweet and sour dipping sauce.

SINGAPORE

SINGAPORE FRIED NOODLES

SERVES 4 • PREPARATION: 20 MINUTES • COOKING: 8 MINUTES

2 tbsp peanut oil
5 oz raw shrimp, peeled
5 oz squid, cleaned
 and cut into rings
1 red onion, peeled
 and sliced
1/2 green bell pepper, seeded
 and cut into strips
1/2 red bell pepper, seeded
 and cut into strips
2 garlic cloves, peeled and
 chopped fine
4 oz beansprouts
1 tbsp mild curry paste
2 tbsp light soy sauce
5 oz fine egg noodles,
 cooked according to the
 package instructions
2 large eggs, beaten
Cilantro leaf, chopped fresh

If fresh egg noodles are available, these can be substituted for dried. Increase the quantity to 9 ounces and add them straight to the wok as they need no pre-cooking.

1   Heat 1 tablespoon peanut oil in a wok, add the shrimp and squid and stir-fry for one minute over a high heat. Remove and set aside.

2   Add the remaining peanut oil to the wok and stir-fry the onion for two minutes. Add the bell peppers and garlic, and stir-fry for two minutes.

3   Add the beansprouts, toss over the heat for 30 seconds, then stir in the curry paste and soy sauce. Stir-fry for one minute, add the noodles, and pour in the eggs. Toss everything together until the egg starts to set, return the seafood to the wok, and stir-fry for one minute.

4   Serve sprinkled with chopped cilantro leaves.

NASI GORENG

SERVES 4 · PREPARATION: 15 MINUTES · COOKING: 10 MINUTES

1 tsp sambal oelek
2 tbsp kecap manis
1 tbsp tomato ketchup
4 tbsp peanut oil
4 scallions, chopped
2 carrots, cut into sticks
4 oz button mushrooms,
  sliced
1 garlic clove, peeled
  and crushed
1 chicken breast, skinned
  and cut into small pieces
4 oz frozen peas
8 oz long grain rice, cooked
4 oz small peeled shrimp
8 cooked jumbo shrimp
1 large egg, beaten

A traditional Indonesian rice dish that has become popular around the world. This version is made with chicken and shrimp, but the chicken can be replaced with pork, firm white fish, or more vegetables.

1   Mix together the sambal oelek, kecap manis, and ketchup.

2   Heat two tablespoons of peanut oil in a wok and stir-fry the scallions and carrots for two minutes over a medium heat. Add the mushrooms and garlic and stir-fry for a further two minutes. Remove from the wok and set aside.

3   Add 1 tablespoon peanut oil to the wok, increase the heat to high, and stir-fry the chicken for two minutes. Return the vegetables to the wok, add the frozen peas, rice, and small shrimp and pour in the sambal oelek mixture.

4   Toss the ingredients together over the heat for three minutes until piping hot. Pile into a serving dish, arrange the jumbo shrimp around, and transfer to a low oven.

5   Heat the remaining peanut oil in a small skillet, add the egg, and cook until it sets as a thin omelet. Tip out of the skillet onto a cutting board and cut into strips. Arrange the omelet strips over the rice mixture in a lattice and serve at once.

CHINA

PORK, CRAB, & MUSHROOM LETTUCE ROLLS

SERVES 4 • PREPARATION: 15 MINUTES • COOKING: 15 MINUTES

2 tbsp peanut oil
10 oz ground pork
1 tsp fresh ginger puree
2 shiitake mushrooms,
  chopped
4 scallions,
  chopped fine
5 oz water chestnuts,
  chopped fine
3 tbsp dark soy sauce
1 tbsp oyster sauce
2 tbsp rice wine
1 tsp sesame oil
4 oz beansprouts
6 oz white crabmeat,
  slivered
8 medium-sized iceberg
  lettuce leaves

To garnish:
Shredded scallions
Cilantro leaves
Shredded red chili

Known as *Sang Chow Bau* in China, these crisp lettuce rolls make a good dish for a buffet party. Serve the hot pork and crab filling in a bowl in the center of a platter with the lettuce around it so guests can spoon the filling into the cup-shaped leaves and roll them up. Iceberg is the ideal lettuce as it has thick, crisp leaves. The easiest way to remove them whole is to hold the lettuce upright under cold running water and carefully peel the leaves away.

1   Heat the peanut oil in a skillet and fry the pork over a medium heat until lightly browned. Add the ginger, shiitake mushrooms, scallions, and water chestnuts and cook for one minute.

2   Add the dark soy sauce, oyster sauce, rice wine, and sesame oil and simmer for three minutes. Add the beansprouts and crabmeat, stir well until mixed in, and cook for two to three minutes.

3   To serve, spoon a little pork mixture into a lettuce cup, add some shredded scallions, cilantro leaves, and shredded chili, roll the lettuce leaf around the filling, and eat with your fingers.

JAPAN

CRAB & VEGETABLE TEMPURA WITH TERIYAKI DIP

SERVES 4–6 • PREPARATION: 15 MINUTES • COOKING: 15 MINUTES

Tempura:
9 oz white crabmeat,
    slivered
1 zucchini, grated
1 carrot, grated
2 scallions, chopped fine
Finely grated zest of 1 lime
2 egg yolks
1¼ cups cold water
1¾ cups all-purpose flour
Peanut oil for
    deep-frying

Teriyaki Dip:
4 tbsp Japanese
    soy sauce
2 tbsp mirin
2 tbsp sake
1 tsp granulated
    brown sugar
2 tbsp chopped cilantro leaf

When deep-frying, it's important to heat the oil to the correct temperature—too hot and the food will burn on the outside before it is cooked in the middle, too cool and the fritters will absorb too much oil and become greasy and soggy. If your deep-fryer does not have a thermostat, inexpensive cooking thermometers can be bought from kitchen stores.

1   In a bowl, mix together the crabmeat, zucchini, carrot, scallions, and lime zest.

2   In another bowl, whisk together the egg yolks with the cold water and gradually stir in the flour. Add the crab and vegetables and stir until well combined.

3   Heat the peanut oil for deep-frying to 350°F. Drop small spoonfuls of the batter mixture into the hot oil and fry in batches for five minutes or until golden brown and crisp. Drain onto paper towels.

4   To make the dip, stir the ingredients together in a small bowl until the sugar dissolves. Serve the hot fritters with the dip.

RICE WINE & RICE VINEGAR

Mirin is a sweet rice wine which is fermented from glutinous rice and distilled rice spirit before being matured for two months to produce its sweet flavor. It is widely used in Japanese dipping sauces and glazes for meat and fish. Sake is also a Japanese rice wine but it is available in many different qualities, and unlike mirin can be served as a drink—the bottle being put in a bucket filled with warm water rather than ice cubes. When used in cooked dishes, the alcohol is always burned or heated off.

The Chinese have brewed rice wine for over four thousand years and today, styles range from mild and fragrant to powerful and sherry-like. The wine from Shao Xing, a district south of Hangzhou, is generally considered to be the finest. Rice vinegar is used extensively in Japanese and Chinese cooking, Chinese being dark brown while Japanese is clear. Drinking rice vinegar mixed with water has been a traditional Japanese hangover cure for centuries.

4 cups chicken broth
1 boneless chicken breast,
  skinned and cut into
  small pieces
7 oz sweet corn kernels
¹/₂ tsp fresh ginger puree
1 tbsp cornstarch
7 oz white crabmeat,
  slivered
3 tbsp rice wine
4 scallions, chopped fine

CHINA

SWEET CORN, CRAB, & CHICKEN SOUP

SERVES 4 • PREPARATION: 10 MINUTES • COOKING: 10 MINUTES

The secret of a good soup is to start with a well-flavored broth, and this is particularly true in Asia where soups are an important part of most meals. Lighter soups are served throughout the meal to cleanse the palate between dishes, but this one is more filling and best served as a first course.

1   Heat the broth in a large saucepan, add the chicken, sweet corn, and ginger, and simmer for five minutes or until the chicken is cooked.

2   Mix the cornstarch with a little water until smooth and stir into the pan. Continue to stir over the heat until the soup thickens.

3   Add the crabmeat and rice wine and cook for one minute. Serve the soup sprinkled with the scallions.

THAILAND

CRAB AND SNOW PEA SALAD

SERVES 4 • PREPARATION: 2 HOURS (PLUS COOLING) • COOKING: 4 MINUTES

2 tbsp peanut oil
6 oz snow peas, thinly sliced
  lengthwise
6 oz baby corn, halved
  lengthwise
¹/₂ red bell pepper, seeded
  and sliced thin
4 oz beansprouts
1 lb white crabmeat
¹/₂ head of Chinese leaves,
  shredded
1 red chili, seeded and
  chopped very fine
¹/₂ tsp fresh ginger puree
8 tbsp sunflower oil
4 tbsp rice vinegar
2 tbsp light soy sauce
1 tsp granulated sugar

Use fresh white crabmeat to make the salad but pick it over carefully first in case any small sharp pieces of shell are hidden in the larger flakes of flesh.

1   Heat the peanut oil in a wok and stir-fry the snow peas, baby corn, and red bell pepper over a medium heat for three minutes.

2   Add the beansprouts and stir-fry for a further minute. Set aside to cool.

3   Break up the crabmeat into large flakes. Divide the Chinese leaves between serving plates, and top with the stir-fried vegetables and then the crab.

4   To make the dressing, whisk the remaining ingredients together until the granulated sugar has dissolved. Pour the dressing over the salad and serve.

RIGHT Sweetcorn, crab, & chicken soup

JAPAN

MIRIN-GLAZED SALMON WITH MIXED VEGETABLES

SERVES 4 • MARINATING: 2 HOURS • PREPARATION: 20 MINUTES • COOKING: 10 MINUTES

Salmon:
2 tbsp mirin
2 tbsp light soy sauce
$^1/_2$ tsp fresh ginger puree
$^1/_2$ tsp sweet chili sauce
Four 5-oz salmon fillets, skinned
1 tsp peanut oil

Mixed vegetables:
2 tbsp peanut oil
4 oz tenderstem broccoli spears
2 sticks of celery, cut into sticks
1 red bell pepper, seeded and sliced thin
8 scallions, sliced
6 oz beansprouts, rinsed
$^1/_2$ cup fish broth

To garnish:
Lime wedges

Before cooking the salmon, ensure the skillet is really hot or the fish will stick and break up when you try and turn the fillets over.

1 Mix together the mirin, light soy sauce, ginger, and chili sauce. Place the salmon fillets in a shallow dish and pour over the mirin mixture. Cover and leave to marinate in a cool place for two hours.

2 Heat a ridged grill pan or heavy skillet and lightly grease with the peanut oil. Add the fish to the skillet and cook for about five minutes, turning over once.

3 Meanwhile stir-fry the vegetables. Heat the peanut oil in a wok, add the broccoli, celery, red bell pepper, and scallions and stir-fry over a high heat for three minutes.

4 Add the beansprouts and any marinade left in the salmon dish and stir-fry for a further two minutes.

5 When the salmon is cooked, remove the fillets from the skillet and keep warm. Add the fish broth to the skillet and let it bubble for one minute, scraping the pan with a spoon to incorporate any cooking juices.

6 Serve the salmon with the vegetables and the pan juices drizzled over. Accompany with lime wedges.

JAPAN

SUKIYAKI WITH STIR-FRIED VEGETABLES

SERVES 4 · PREPARATION: 15 MINUTES · COOKING: 10 MINUTES

4 tbsp peanut oil

12 shiitake mushrooms, halved or quartered

2 heads of bok choy, sliced thin and coarse stalks discarded

4 oz canned bamboo shoots, sliced

8 scallions, sliced

1¼ lb fillet or rump steak, sliced thin across the grain of the meat

1 garlic clove, peeled and sliced thin

1-in piece of gingerroot, peeled and grated or chopped fine

2 tbsp Japanese soy sauce

2 tbsp mirin

1 tbsp rice vinegar

2 tbsp sesame seeds

The Japanese would use a special pot similar to an electric wok or skillet to cook Sukiyaki at the table but this variation can be prepared in the kitchen and served to guests in the normal way. Good quality tender beef is essential as the meat is only seared—in Japan the famous Kobe beef would be the first choice of most chefs.

1   Heat half the peanut oil in a wok and stir-fry the shiitake mushrooms and bok choy for two minutes over a fairly brisk heat. Add the bamboo shoots and scallions and stir-fry for a further two minutes. Remove the vegetables from the wok and keep warm.

2   Add the remaining peanut oil to the wok and turn up the heat. Fry the steak slices in batches for one to two minutes until they are browned on both sides but still pink in the center. When you have browned the meat, return all the slices to the wok and pour in the Japanese soy sauce, mirin, and rice vinegar.

3   Allow to simmer until the steak slices are coated in a sticky glaze. Sprinkle over the sesame seeds and serve with the stir-fried vegetables.

VIETNAM

WARM SALMON & SHRIMP SALAD

SERVES 4 · MARINATING: 1–2 HOURS · PREPARATION: 20 MINUTES · COOKING: 2 MINUTES

6 oz salmon fillet, skinned
  and cut into chunks or
  thin slices
6 oz raw tiger shrimp,
  peeled

Marinade:
3 tbsp Japanese soy sauce
2 tbsp mirin
1 tsp sesame oil

Salad vegetables:
4 oz white radish
  (daikon), grated or
  cut into thin sticks
4 oz carrot, grated or
  cut into thin sticks
2 sticks of celery, sliced thin
1 oz alfalfa sprouts

Dressing:
4 tbsp sunflower oil
2 tbsp rice vinegar
2 tbsp Japanese soy sauce
1 tbsp mirin

Serve the salad while the salmon and shrimp are still warm on a bed of baby spinach leaves or shredded iceberg lettuce.

1 Put the salmon and shrimp in a bowl. Mix together the marinade ingredients, pour over the salmon and shrimp, and stir until they are coated. Cover and leave in a cool place to marinate for one to two hours.

2 Divide the salad vegetables between four serving plates. To make the dressing, whisk together half the sunflower oil with the rice vinegar, Japanese soy sauce, and mirin.

3 Heat the remaining sunflower oil in a wok and stir-fry the salmon and shrimp over a fairly high heat for two minutes until just cooked. Add any marinade left in the bowl, allow it to simmer and coat the salmon and shrimp, then spoon on top of the vegetables.

4 Pour over the dressing and serve at once.

2 duck breasts, skin on
2 tbsp and 1 tsp peanut oil
1 red bell pepper, seeded
and sliced
2 oz beansprouts
3 oz mushrooms, sliced
2 oz fresh water chestnuts,
rinsed and chopped
3 tbsp rice vinegar
1 tbsp clear honey
3 tbsp light soy sauce
2 tbsp tomato ketchup
4 eggs

CHINA

OMELET ROLLS WITH SWEET & SOUR DUCK

SERVES 4 · PREPARATION: 20 MINUTES (PLUS STANDING) · COOKING: 20 MINUTES

Water chestnuts can be bought fresh or canned. Canned are more convenient as fresh ones (*see* left) need to be peeled before cooking, whereas canned chesnuts are ready-prepared.

1 Grill the duck breasts for about 10 minutes or until almost cooked, turning once or twice. Transfer to a board, leave them to stand for five minutes, and then carve into thin slices, discarding the skin if you prefer.

2 Heat 2 tablespoons peanut oil in a wok, add the red bell pepper and stir-fry for three minutes over a fairly high heat. Add the beansprouts, mushrooms, and water chestnuts and stir-fry for two minutes.

3 Mix together the rice vinegar, clear honey, light soy sauce, and tomato ketchup and pour into the wok. Add the duck and toss until the ingredients are coated in the sauce. Leave over a low heat while you cook the omelets.

4 Heat 1 teaspoon peanut oil in a small (roughly 7 ins in diameter) skillet. Beat one egg and pour into the skillet, tilting it so the egg covers the base. Cook until the egg has just set, and remove from the skillet. Make three more omelets in the same way.

5 Divide the duck and vegetables between the omelets and roll up. Cut into slices and serve with soy sauce for dipping.

CHINA

BABY BOK CHOY WITH GARLIC & STRAW MUSHROOMS

SERVES 4 • PREPARATION: 10 MINUTES • COOKING: 5 MINUTES

1 lb baby bok choy
1 tbsp peanut oil
**2 garlic cloves, chopped
 and sliced thin**
**4 oz straw mushrooms,
 halved**
2 tbsp rice wine
Pinch of granulated sugar
Pinch of salt

Native to China, straw mushrooms grow mainly in the south of the country where they are cultivated on beds of rice straw, hence their name. They are available in cans from Asian food stores, and need to be drained and rinsed before use.

1 Blanch the bok choy in a saucepan of boiling water for one minute. Drain, and cool by running cold water over the leaves.

2 Heat the peanut oil in a wok, add the garlic and fry gently for one minute until golden. Drain from the wok and set aside. Add the straw mushrooms and bok choy and stir-fry over a high heat for two minutes. Add the rice wine, sugar, and salt, and stir until the vegetables are coated in the wok juices.

3 Transfer to a serving plate, spoon over the garlic and serve at once.

JAPAN

TERIYAKI ROAST CHICKEN

SERVES 4 • MARINATING: 4 HOURS • PREPARATION: 10 MINUTES • COOKING: 5 MINUTES

4 chicken breasts, skinned
4 tbsp Japanese soy sauce
4 tbsp mirin
2 tbsp sake
1 tbsp granulated
   brown sugar

Teriyaki is a Japanese sauce of mirin, sake, brown sugar, and Japanese soy sauce which reduces down to a shiny, sweet glaze to coat grilled or barbecued chicken, fish, shellfish, or meat. Marinate the chicken before cooking so it has time to absorb the flavors of the teriyaki mix.

1   Slice the flesh of the chicken breasts at ½-in intervals with a sharp knife without cutting all the way through.

2   Place the chicken breasts in a shallow dish side by side. Mix together the soy sauce, mirin, sake, and brown sugar, stirring until the sugar dissolves. Pour over the chicken, turning the breasts over so they are well coated, cover, and leave in a cool place to marinate for four hours or longer.

3   Lift the chicken breasts from the marinade and grill or barbecue for five minutes on each side or until cooked through, brushing with any glaze left in the dish as they cook.

4   Serve the chicken hot, cut into slices, and accompany with salad.

KOREA

GLAZED PUMPKIN

SERVES 4 (AS A SIDE DISH) • PREPARATION: 15 MINUTES • COOKING: 20 MINUTES

1½ lb pumpkin
1 red onion, peeled and
    sliced fine
2 large garlic cloves, peeled
    and chopped fine
2 tbsp peanut oil
2 tbsp rice vinegar
2 tbsp water
2 oz granulated
    brown sugar
1 tsp fresh ginger puree
6 tbsp Japanese soy sauce

In Korea, a selection of salads and vegetable side dishes known as *panchan* are served to accompany main courses of meat, poultry, and fish. Pumpkin would most likely be used in Korea where it is a popular vegetable, but the sticky, spicy rice vinegar and ginger glaze works equally well with butternut squash.

1   Preheat the oven to 375°F.

2   Cut the pumpkin in half, scoop out the seeds, and peel. Cut the flesh into thick slices or chop into 1½-in chunks. Place in a bowl and mix with the red onion, garlic, and peanut oil.

3   Tip out the pumpkin into a shallow roasting pan and spread it out. Roast in the oven for 15 minutes or until the pumpkin is almost tender.

4   Mix together the rice vinegar, water, brown sugar, ginger puree, and Japanese soy sauce, stirring until the sugar dissolves. Spoon the glazeover the pumpkin, turning the pieces over until coated. Return to the oven for a further 10 minutes or until the squash is tender and glazed with the rice vinegar and ginger mixture.

THAILAND

BBQ CHICKEN WITH CHILI VINEGAR SAUCE

SERVES 4 • MARINATING: 2 HOURS • PREPARATION: 15 MINUTES (PLUS COOLING)
COOKING: 20 MINUTES

Chicken:

4 boneless chicken breasts,
  skin still on
2 tbsp light soy sauce
1 tbsp fish sauce
1 tsp granulated
  brown sugar
2 garlic cloves, peeled
  and crushed
1 tsp fresh chili puree
1 tbsp peanut oil

Sauce:

6 tbsp rice vinegar
2 tbsp granulated
  brown sugar
$^1/_2$ tsp fresh ginger puree
1 red chili, seeded and
  chopped fine
1 tbsp light soy sauce

If it is not the right time of year for a barbecue, the chicken can be cooked under a conventional grill or in a ridged hob-top pan. Serve with Thai sticky rice or stir-fried rice as you prefer.

1 Place the chicken breasts side by side in a shallow dish. Mix together the light soy sauce, fish sauce, brown sugar, garlic, chili puree, and peanut oil, stirring until the sugar dissolves.

2 Pour the soy sauce mix over the chicken, turning the breasts over so they are well coated. Cover and leave to marinate in a cool place for two hours or longer.

3 To make the sauce, heat the rice vinegar and sugar gently in a pan until the sugar dissolves. Simmer for two minutes, then remove from the heat and stir in the ginger puree, red chili, and light soy sauce. Allow to cool.

4 Lift the chicken from the marinade and barbecue for 10 to 15 minutes until cooked through, brushing with any marinade left in the dish. Cut each chicken breast into three or four thick slices and serve with the sauce spooned over.

JAPAN

SUSHI BENTO BOX

SERVES 6 • PREPARATION: 45 MINUTES (PLUS STANDING) • COOKING: 8 MINUTES

11 oz sushi rice
5 tbsp rice vinegar
2 tbsp granulated sugar
1 tsp sesame oil
1 tsp salt
5–6 sheets dried
    nori seaweed
Cooked peeled shrimp,
    cucumber, carrot, red bell
    pepper, scallion slices,
    wafer thin slices of
    smoked salmon and sushi
    grade tuna, sesame seeds,
    or chives

To serve:
Green wasabi paste
Japanese soy sauce
Pink pickled ginger

The number one choice in Japan for a quick lunch, bento boxes are small wooden, lacquered boxes filled with delicious morsels of sushi rice topped with shrimp, sashimi, or chopped vegetables, or wrapped in thin sheets of nori seaweed. Bought from street vendors and served with soy sauce, pickled ginger, and a squeeze of fiery wasabi, they are the ultimate in chic fast food.

1   Put the sushi rice in a sieve and run cold water through it until the water is clear. Drain well and put in a saucepan. Add 11 fl oz boiling water, cover, and simmer gently for eight minutes. Turn off the heat and leave to stand covered for 15 minutes.

2   Mix the rice vinegar and granulated sugar together, stirring until the sugar dissolves. Add the sesame oil and salt, mix well, and pour onto the hot rice. Transfer the rice to a shallow dish, and turn over with a spatula until it has cooled.

3   Place a nori sheet onto a sushi mat and spread two-thirds of the surface with an even layer of rice. Add shrimp, sliced cucumber, carrot, red bell pepper or scallion slices and roll the sheet up, tucking the uncovered part of the nori inside and dampening the final edge to stick it down. Cut the roll into six pieces using a damp knife.

4   Make other sushi rolls in the same way, or shape rice into small rectangles and top with smoked salmon, shrimp, tuna slices, chives, and sesame seeds.

5   Serve with green wasabi paste, Japanese soy sauce, and pink pickled ginger.

JAPAN

GREEN TEA & MIRIN ICE CREAM WITH RED BEAN SAUCE

SERVES 6 • PREPARATION: 30 MINUTES (PLUS FREEZING) • COOKING: 10 MINUTES

Ice cream:
2½ cups double cream
1 tbsp powdered green tea
½ cup icing sugar
2 tbsp mirin
3 large egg yolks

Red bean sauce:
3 oz red bean paste
1 tbsp sake
½ cup water

To serve:
Fresh fruit, such as raspberries, cape gooseberries

Use powdered green tea rather than leaves or a tea bag to give this unusual ice cream its vivid color. Red bean paste is made from crushed adzuki beans and is available from Asian grocery stores.

1 To make the ice cream, stir a little of the cream into the tea in a bowl until smooth. Heat the rest of the cream in a saucepan, and as it comes to a boil, pour it onto the tea mixture, stirring until blended.

2 Whisk the icing sugar, mirin, and egg yolks together until creamy. Slowly whisk in the hot tea mixture and then strain back into the saucepan.

3 Cook over a low heat, without letting the mixture boil, until it coats the back of a spoon. Allow to cool and then pour into a plastic container and freeze.

4 To make the sauce, mix the paste with the sake in a saucepan, and gradually stir in the water. Stir over a low heat until boiling. Allow to cool and then chill until ready to serve.

5 Serve the ice cream in scoops with the sauce accompanied by fresh fruit.

COCONUT

Coconut is widely used in Thailand, Vietnam, Indonesia, and the Malay Peninsula, particularly for making soups and curry sauces. Freshly grated flesh from young coconuts is added to both main and dessert dishes, as are coconut milk and cream, which are available in cans, cartons, or in a block. Asian recipe books will often call for "young coconut juice"—this is not the sweet liquid inside a newly picked coconut but the flesh blended with hot water and then strained through a fine sieve. Coconut oil is also traditionally used for cooking in Indonesia.

INDONESIAN SATAY WITH SPICY PEANUT SAUCE

SERVES 4 · MARINATING: 5 HOURS · PREPARATION: 25 MINUTES · COOKING: 10 MINUTES

Satay:
2 garlic cloves, peeled and crushed
4 tbsp kecap manis
Juice of 2 limes
4 boneless chicken breasts, skinned and cut into strips
2 tbsp peanut oil

Sauce:
1 tbsp peanut oil
2 shallots, peeled and chopped fine
$^1/_4$ tsp trassi
4 tbsp crunchy peanut butter
1 tbsp kecap manis
Juice of 1 lime
1 tsp sambal oelek
$^3/_4$ cup coconut milk
1 tbsp chopped cilantro leaf

This is one of Southeast Asia's most popular snack foods, and streets lined with barbecues piled high with roasting satays are a familiar sight in cities like Singapore. The most common accompaniment is a peanut and coconut sauce, but other dips such as chili sauce (*see* page 40) can be substituted.

1 To make the satay, mix together the garlic, sweet soy sauce, and lime juice. Thread the chicken onto skewers, place in a single layer in a shallow dish, and spoon the garlic mixture over the meat. Leave in a cool place to marinate for several hours, turning the skewers over occasionally.

2 Transfer the skewers to a foil-lined grill pan and drizzle the peanut oil over the chicken.

3 To make the sauce, heat the peanut oil in a pan and fry the shallots for three to four minutes over a gentle heat until softened but not browned. Add the trassi, breaking it up with the back of a spoon.

4 Add the peanut butter, kecap manis, lime juice, and sambal oelek and when well mixed, gradually stir in the coconut milk. Simmer gently while you cook the satays.

5 Grill the satays for three to four minutes, turning the skewers over half way until the chicken is well browned. Scatter the cilantro leaf over the sauce and serve.

SAFFRON ANGLER FISH STEAMED IN BANANA LEAVES

SERVES 4 • PREPARATION: 10 MINUTES (PLUS COOLING) • COOKING: 15 MINUTES

4 tbsp coconut cream or thick coconut milk

Few strands of saffron, crumbled

1 lb angler fish fillet, skinned and minced

1 tsp granulated sugar

1 red chili, seeded and chopped fine

1 tsp fresh lemon grass puree

1 egg, beaten

8 fresh banana leaves, measuring roughly 6 in square

Banana leaves are available from the chiller or freezer cabinets of Asian food stores, but sheets of aluminum foil work equally well. The ribs running down the leaves make them fragile and liable to split if not handled with care.

1 Warm the coconut cream and saffron gently in a small skillet until almost boiling. Remove from the heat and set aside to cool.

2 Put the minced fish in a bowl and stir in the sugar, red chili, lemon grass puree, coconut cream, saffron, and beaten egg, mixing well.

3 Dip the banana leaves in hot water for a few seconds to soften them and make them easier to fold. Spread them out on the work surface and divide the fish mixture between the leaves. Wrap the leaves around the filling and secure with string or cocktail sticks.

4 Place the parcels in a steamer and steam for 15 minutes until firm. Serve immediately, leaving diners to unwrap the parcels themselves.

MALAYSIA

CHICKEN WITH MANGO & COCONUT SAUCE

SERVES 4 • PREPARATION: 25 MINUTES • COOKING: 15 MINUTES

Ripe mangoes will give this dish a deliciously aromatic taste. If the creamed coconut has hardened in the pack, chop or grate it before adding to the sauce.

2 medium-sized
  ripe mangoes
1¼ cups chicken broth
Juice of 1 lime
2 tbsp light soy sauce
6 sprigs of fresh cilantro
1 red chile, seeded
  and sliced
1 tsp fresh galangal puree
4 chicken breasts, cut
  into 2-in pieces
16 asparagus spears
2 oz creamed coconut

1 Peel the mangoes and cut the flesh away from the fibrous center stone. Place in a food processor and reduce to a puree.

2 Put the broth, lime juice, light soy sauce, cilantro sprigs, red chile, and galangal puree in a wok and bring to simmering point.

3 Lay the chicken and asparagus on a rack and place in the wok. Cover and steam for 10 minutes or until the chicken is cooked and the asparagus spears are tender. Remove the chicken and asparagus to a plate and keep warm in a low oven.

4 Strain the cooking liquid from the wok into a jug. Pour the pureed mango into the wok and add the creamed coconut. Heat until almost boiling, then stir in enough of the cooking liquid to make a fairly thick sauce. Simmer for one to two minutes.

5 Divide the chicken and asparagus between serving plates and spoon over the sauce. Serve with rice.

MALAYSIA

CHICKEN & SHRIMP LAKSA

SERVES 4 • PREPARATION: 15 MINUTES • COOKING: 10 MINUTES

Laksa makes a popular mid-morning snack in the Malay peninsula, although in the West we would probably prefer it at lunch or supper time. The ingredients can vary enormously, so feel free to add other vegetables, fish instead of chicken, and egg noodles in place of flat rice ones according to what you have available.

4 tbsp peanut oil
4 red shallots, peeled
  and sliced fine
2 garlic cloves, peeled
  and crushed
1 tsp fresh lemon grass
  puree
1/2 tsp trassi
1 red chili, seeded and
  chopped fine
1 tbsp ground coriander
2 1/2 cups chicken broth
1 3/4 cups coconut milk
1 tbsp granulated
  brown sugar
2 boneless chicken breasts,
  cut into bite-size pieces
11 oz raw tiger
  shrimp, peeled
9 oz fresh flat rice noodles
6 oz snow peas, sliced
4 oz beansprouts

To garnish:
Chopped scallions
1 red chili, chopped fine

1   Heat half the peanut oil in a large saucepan and fry the shallots over a gentle heat until softened.

2   Add the garlic, lemon grass puree, trassi, red chili, and coriander and continue to cook gently for two to three minutes.

3   Stir in the chicken broth, coconut milk, and sugar and bring to a simmer. Add the chicken, tiger shrimp, and noodles and leave over a low heat.

4   Heat the remaining peanut oil in a wok and stir-fry the snow peas and beansprouts for two minutes or until they start to soften.

5   Spoon the laksa into serving dishes and stir in the snow peas and beansprouts. Serve garnished with the scallions and chili.

THAILAND

RED VEGETABLE CURRY WITH SQUASH & SWEET POTATO

SERVES 4 • PREPARATION: 25 MINUTES • COOKING: 30 MINUTES

2 tbsp peanut oil

2 tbsp red Thai curry paste

1 red onion, peeled
   and sliced

1 sweet potato, peeled and
   cut into ³/₄-in dice

7 oz butternut squash,
   peeled, seeded and cut
   into ³/₄-in dice

1 green bell pepper, seeded
   and chopped

1 zucchini, chopped

4 oz shiitake mushrooms,
   sliced

2 tbsp Thai fish sauce

1 tbsp lime juice

2 tsp granulated
   brown sugar

1 tsp lemon grass, sliced fine

1¹/₂ cups coconut milk

To garnish:

1 tbsp red onion,
   chopped fine

1 red chili, seeded
   and chopped fine

2 tbsp shredded
   fresh coconut or
   desiccated coconut

Cut the squash and sweet potato into small pieces so they cook quickly and evenly. The curry can be served on its own as a vegetarian meal or as an accompaniment to a spicy meat or fish dish.

1 Heat the peanut oil in a deep skillet or large saucepan, add the Thai curry paste and onion and fry over a low heat for two to three minutes until the onion starts to soften.

2 Add the sweet potato and butternut squash and fry for a further 10 minutes, stirring occasionally.

3 Add the green bell pepper, zucchini, and shiitake mushrooms, fry for two minutes, then add the Thai fish sauce, lime juice, sugar, lemon grass, and coconut milk.

4 Cover the pan and leave the curry to simmer gently for 10 to 15 minutes or until the vegetables are tender. Garnish with the red onion, red chili, and coconut. Serve with boiled rice.

GOLDEN COCONUT CHICKEN

SERVES 4 • PREPARATION: 15 MINUTES (PLUS STANDING) • COOKING: 20 MINUTES

¹/₂ tsp saffron threads

2 tbsp peanut oil

4 chicken breasts, each
   cut into 3 or 4 pieces

3 red shallots, peeled
   and sliced fine

2 zucchini, chopped

4 oz button mushrooms,
   halved

2 tsp ground coriander

2 garlic cloves, peeled
   and crushed

1 tsp fresh ginger puree

1³/₄ cups coconut milk

2 tbsp chopped cilantro leaf

Adding saffron to the coconut sauce gives it a rich golden hue. Before soaking, crumble the saffron threads between your fingers—this will release all their vivid color and aroma.

1   Crumble the saffron threads into a small bowl and pour over boiling water to just cover. Leave to stand for 10 minutes.

2   Heat the peanut oil in a wok and stir-fry the chicken pieces in two batches over a high heat for two to three minutes until lightly browned. Remove from the wok and set aside.

3   Add the shallots, zucchini, and button mushrooms to the wok and stir-fry over a medium heat for five minutes. Add the ground coriander, garlic, and ginger puree and fry for one minute.

4   Pour in the coconut milk and the saffron threads with their soaking water, and return the chicken to the wok. Simmer gently over a low heat for 10 minutes or until the chicken is cooked. Serve with the chopped cilantro scattered over, and accompany with steamed or boiled rice.

SINGAPORE

ROASTED COCONUT & CHILI FISH

SERVES 4 · PREPARATION: 10 MINUTES · COOKING: 8–9 MINUTES

Four 6-oz firm fish fillets such as swordfish, marlin, angler fish, or tuna
¹/₂ tsp chili paste
1 tbsp finely chopped cilantro leaves
¹/₂ tsp fresh ginger puree
³/₄ cup coconut cream
Juice of 1 lime

Any firm-fleshed fish fillets would be suitable for this recipe—swordfish or marlin work particularly well.

1   Line the grill pan with foil and place the fish fillets on it side by side. Grill for three to four minutes.

2   Meanwhile, mix together the chili paste, cilantro, ginger puree, and coconut cream. Turn the fish fillets over and spoon the coconut mixture on top.

3   Squeeze over the lime juice and grill for a further five minutes or until the fish is cooked and the topping lightly scorched.

THAILAND

COCONUT CUSTARD WITH STAR ANISE

SERVES 4 · PREPARATION: 15 MINUTES · COOKING: 25 MINUTES

2 large eggs, lightly beaten
2 oz superfine sugar
1¹/₄ cups thick canned coconut milk
¹/₄ tsp ground star anise

Sankhaya is a creamy Thai custard made with coconut milk and steamed in small dishes. When making the custard, take care not to let it boil or it will separate. If this does happen, remove it from the heat and strain or blend in a food processor to make it smooth again.

1   Whisk the eggs and sugar together until creamy. Gradually stir in the coconut milk and ground star anise until blended.

2   Strain the mixture into a double boiler or into a bowl set over a pan of simmering water. Cook over a low heat, stirring continuously, until the custard is thick enough to coat the back of a wooden spoon.

3   Pour the custard into four ramekins, cover with foil, and steam over gently simmering water for 15 minutes or until the custards are just set.

4   Leave to cool and then chill until ready to serve.

CHINA

MANGO & COCONUT MOUSSE

SERVES 6 • PREPARATION. 15 MINUTES (PLUS SOAKING AND SETTING)

1 lb ripe mangoes
¹/₂ cup coconut cream
4 sheets of leaf gelatine
²/₃ cup pineapple
   or lychee juice

To serve:
Mint leaves
Red bean sauce
   (*see* **page 98**)

Leaf gelatine is easier to dissolve than the powdered variety, which can leave granules or unpleasant lumps of jelly in the finished dish. Powdered gelatine can be used if you find it easier to obtain—use a tablespoon of powdered in place of four sheets.

1 Peel the mangoes and carefully cut the flesh away from the fibrous center stone. Put the flesh in a food processor, add the coconut cream, and blend to a puree. Transfer to a bowl.

2 Soak the gelatine leaves in a little cold water for five minutes to soften. Remove and squeeze them out.

3 Heat the pineapple or lychee juice until almost boiling, add the gelatine leaves, and stir until they dissolve. Stir the gelatine mixture into the mango puree, transfer to a bowl, and chill until set.

4 Serve with fresh mint leaves and red bean sauce (*see* page 98).

BANANA & PINEAPPLE FRITTERS IN COCONUT BATTER

SERVES 4 · PREPARATION: 20 MINUTES (PLUS STANDING) · COOKING: 10 MINUTES

1 cup all-purpose flour, plus
    extra for dusting
$1/2$ tsp ground ginger
2 oz superfine sugar
1 cup coconut milk
Peanut oil for
    deep-frying
2 bananas, peeled and
    cut into 2-in lengths
2 pineapple rings, quartered

To serve:
Shredded young coconut
    or desiccated coconut

If using canned pineapple, drain it well and blot away any juice with a paper towel before coating with the batter. Use slightly under-ripe bananas so they do not become too soft when cooked.

1   Sift the flour and ginger into a bowl and stir in the superfine sugar. Make a well in the center of the dry ingredients and pour in the coconut milk. Whisk to make a smooth batter, and then set aside for 30 minutes.

2   Heat the peanut oil to 350°F for deep-frying.

3   Dust the banana and pineapple pieces with flour, dip in the batter until coated, and deep-fry in batches for two to three minutes until golden and crisp. Drain on a paper towel and serve scattered with shredded young coconut or desiccated coconut.

THAILAND

COCONUT STICKY RICE WITH MANGO, PAPAYA, & LIME

SERVES 4 · PREPARATION: 15 MINUTES (PLUS STANDING) · COOKING: 20–25 MINUTES

7 oz sticky rice
3/4 cup coconut milk
1 mango, peeled
   and chopped
1/2 papaya, peeled, seeded
   and chopped
Juice of 2 limes

Also known as "glutinous rice," sticky rice has short white grains and is sold in Asian food stores.

1 Put the sticky rice in a bowl and pour over cold water to cover by two inches. Leave the rice to soak for several hours or overnight.

2 Drain the rice and transfer to a steamer lined with muslin, spreading the grains out.

3 Steam for 20 to 25 minutes until the rice is tender. Warm the coconut milk and mix with the rice. Leave to stand for 15 minutes before serving with the mango and papaya, squeezing the lime juice over the fruit.

4 sheets of leaf gelatine
³/₄ cup coconut milk
³/₄ cup water
¹/₄ cup superfine sugar
2 oz young coconut, grated

To serve:
Toasted fresh or
desiccated coconut

THAILAND

COCONUT JELLY

MAKES 20 · PREPARATION: 15 MINUTES (PLUS SOAKING & SETTING)

Packs of grated young coconut can be found in the freezer cabinet of Asian stores. Serve this in small pieces as it is rich and sweet.

1 Soak the gelatine leaves in a little cold water for five minutes to soften. Remove and squeeze them out.

2 Heat the coconut milk, water, and sugar in a pan until almost boiling, add the gelatine leaves and stir until dissolved.

3 Add the grated coconut, pour into a shallow tray lined with all-purpose plastic wrap, and allow to cool. Chill until set.

4 Serve the jelly cut into small triangles, squares, or flower shapes using a fluted cutter, and scatter with toasted fresh or desiccated coconut.

LEMON GRASS

Lemon grass is a lemon-scented plant whose roots grow in clumps with only the bottom part of the stem being used. When adding to dishes, the coarse outer leaves of the stems should be stripped off and discarded before the softer inner leaves are ground to a paste with a little oil, or sliced thin. Available fresh or as a puree, a teaspoon of ready-prepared puree is equal to one stalk. The fresh stalks make excellent kebob skewers as they infuse the food threaded on them with their delicate flavor. You can also make a lemon grass "brush" for adding flavor for glazing food for barbecuing or grilling—cut a stalk in half to within half an inch of the root and bat it out carefully with a rolling pin.

MALAYSIA

AROMATIC SEAFOOD BROTH

SERVES 4 · PREPARATION: 20 MINUTES · COOKING: 10 MINUTES

When making the broth, do not let the mixture boil for too long or the coconut milk will separate. Simmer the milk over a gentle heat so that it absorbs the flavor of the spices and vegetables and it makes a delicious sauce for the seafood.

1 Put the coconut milk, lemon grass, fish sauce, galangal, mushrooms, lime juice, granulated sugar, and snow peas in a wok or deep skillet and simmer gently for 10 minutes.

2 When the broth is almost ready, heat the peanut oil in another skillet and cook the seafood for two to three minutes until the lobster tails and shrimp turn pink and the squid, angler fish, and scallops opaque.

3 Divide the seafood between serving dishes and spoon the broth over. Garnish with the cilantro leaves and serve with lime wedges to squeeze over the seafood.

1¹/₂ cups coconut milk
2 lemon grass stalks, cut
   into 2-in lengths
1 tbsp fish sauce
1 tsp galangal puree or
   grated fresh root
4 oz mushrooms, sliced or
   quartered
Juice of 1 lime
1 tsp granulated sugar
2 oz snow peas, halved
   lengthwise
2 tbsp peanut oil
2 lobster tails, halved
   lengthwise
8 raw jumbo shrimp, halved
   and deveined
6 oz squid, cleaned, cut into
   bite-size pieces and
   scored
6 oz angler fish fillet, cut
   into bite-size pieces
8 scallops
1 tbsp fresh cilantro leaves

MARINATED TUNA IN A LEMON GRASS VINAIGRETTE

SERVES 4 · PREPARATION: 10 MINUTES (PLUS CHILLING & STANDING)

14 oz fresh sushi-grade tuna
2 red shallots, peeled and
    chopped fine
6 mint leaves,
    sliced very fine

Vinaigrette:
3 tbsp light soy sauce
3 tbsp lime juice
1 tbsp granulated sugar
1 stalk lemon grass,
    sliced fine

To garnish:
Mint leaves

Look for sushi-grade tuna as it means it will be really fresh. To make the fish easier to slice, wrap it tightly in plastic wrap and leave it to chill in the fridge for a couple of hours so that it firms up. To slice, use a non-serrated carving knife with a long, thin blade and cut through the tuna using a sawing motion.

1   Slice the tuna as thinly as possible and arrange on a serving platter. Scatter over the shallots and sliced mint leaves.

2   Mix the vinaigrette ingredients together, stirring until the granulated sugar dissolves, and spoon over the tuna slices.

3   Leave to stand for 15 minutes before serving. Garnish with mint leaves.

STEAMED SHRIMP WITH LEMON GRASS

SERVES 4 · PREPARATION: 15 MINUTES · COOKING: 15 MINUTES

1 lb raw jumbo shrimp
1 stalk of lemon grass,
    quartered lengthwise
8 scallions, trimmed
    and sliced
2 tbsp coarsely chopped
    fresh cilantro leaves
1 red chili, seeded and sliced
    thin

Sauce:
2 tbsp Thai fish sauce
1 tsp granulated sugar
2 tbsp light soy sauce
$^1/_2$ lemon grass stalk,
    sliced thin

A light but aromatic dish that will appeal to anyone counting calories. Skinned chicken breasts can also be cooked using the same method below.

1   Peel the shrimp and cut down the back of each one to remove the dark thread running down its length.

2   Place the lemon grass in a steamer and arrange the shrimp, scallions, cilantro, and red chile on top. Cover and steam over a saucepan of boiling water for five minutes or until the shrimp turn pink.

3   To make the sauce, mix together the Thai fish sauce, granulated sugar, light soy sauce, and lemon grass until the sugar dissolves.

4   Lift the shrimp, scallions, cilantro, and red chile from the steamer and discard the lemon grass. Serve while still hot with the sauce spooned over.

LEFT Marinated tuna in a lemon grass vinaigrette

LEMON GRASS SHRIMP STICKS

SERVES 4 • PREPARATION: 30 MINUTES • GRILLING: 5 MINUTES • STEAMING: 6–7 MINUTES

9 oz raw shrimp, peeled and minced or chopped fine
1 tsp granulated sugar
1 green chili, seeded and chopped fine
1 shallot, peeled and chopped very fine
1 tbsp chopped fresh cilantro leaf
Eight 4-in lemon grass stalks
2 tbsp peanut oil (if grilling)

Dipping sauce:
2 tbsp rice vinegar
1 stalk of lemon grass, chopped fine
2 tbsp fish sauce
1 tsp granulated sugar
1 garlic clove, peeled and chopped fine

The lemon grass infuses the shrimp mixture with its delicate aroma, while the green chili adds an extra kick. The sticks can be steamed or pan-grilled as you prefer.

1   Put the minced shrimp in a bowl and mix in the granulated sugar, green chili, shallot, and chopped cilantro.

2   Divide the mixture into eight and mould each portion around a lemon grass stalk, creating the shrimp sticks.

3   If grilling, heat a heavy ridged grill pan until very hot, brush the shrimp mixture with the peanut oil, and cook for about five minutes until the shrimp mix is firm and opaque, turning the sticks over carefully once or twice. If steaming, place the sticks in a steamer over a saucepan of boiling water, cover and steam for six to seven minutes until the shrimp mixture is cooked.

4   To make the sauce, mix the ingredients together, stirring until the sugar dissolves. Serve the hot shrimp sticks with the dipping sauce.

CHICKEN WITH GOLDEN COCONUT & LEMON GRASS SAUCE

SERVES 4 • PREPARATION: 20 MINUTES • COOKING: 20 MINUTES

6 pink shallots, peeled and chopped

1 large red chili, seeded and chopped

2 garlic cloves, peeled and chopped

1 stalk of lemon grass, chopped

1-in piece of gingerroot, peeled and chopped

2 tbsp peanut oil

1 tsp ground turmeric

1 cup coconut milk

Juice of 1 lime

$^2/_3$ cup chicken broth

4 chicken breasts, skinned and each one cut into 4 pieces

2 kaffir lime leaves, cut into wafer-thin slices

The dish could also be made using medium-sized raw shrimp or firm white fish fillets but they will only need to be simmered for 8 to 10 minutes because they will cook much more quickly than the chicken.

1 Place the shallots, red chili, garlic, lemon grass, gingerroot, and half the peanut oil in a food processor and blend to a paste.

2 Heat the remaining peanut oil in a wok, add the turmeric and the paste, and fry for five minutes over a fairly low heat until the shallots have softened and the paste is aromatic.

3 Gradually stir in the coconut milk, lime juice, and broth and heat until bubbling. Add the chicken and lime leaves and simmer gently for 15 minutes or until the chicken is cooked.

4 Serve with rice or noodles.

6-in piece of fresh lotus root
Peanut oil for
    deep-frying

Dip:
2 tbsp light soy sauce
1 tbsp fish sauce
1 tsp lemon grass, sliced
    very fine
1 tbsp rice vinegar
$^{1}/_{2}$ tsp granulated sugar
1 red chili, seeded and sliced
    fine

CHINA

LOTUS ROOT CHIPS WITH CHILE & LEMON GRASS DIP

SERVES 4 • PREPARATION: 15 MINUTES • COOKING: 10 MINUTES

Lotus root is the root of the Chinese lotus or water lily which grows in ponds and lakes and has a crunchy texture and attractive lace-like appearance. Fry the chips in fairly small batches so any moisture in the lotus root does not lower the temperature of the oil. If you find any that are not as crisp as you would like, raise the temperature of the oil slightly and return them to the pan for a second frying in the same way as you would if you were cooking french fries.

1   Peel the lotus root and slice as thinly as possible using the slicing blade on a food processor or a very sharp knife. Pat any moisture from the slices with paper towels.

2   Heat the peanut oil for deep-frying to 350°F. Fry the slices in batches for one to two minutes until pale golden and crisp.

3   Drain on paper towels and serve with the dip.

4   To make the dip, mix all the ingredients together in a small bowl, stirring until the granulated sugar dissolves.

THAILAND

PORK BALLS ON LEMON GRASS SKEWERS

SERVES 4 · PREPARATION: 30 MINUTES (PLUS CHILLING) · COOKING TIME: 10 MINUTES

1/2 tsp fresh galangal puree
2 tbsp chopped fresh
   cilantro leaf
2 red shallots, peeled and
   chopped very fine
1 lb lean minced pork
Finely grated zest and juice
   of 1 lime
1 egg, beaten
6 lemon grass stalks halved
   lengthwise
2 tbsp peanut oil
1/2 tsp red chili pepper

Dampen your hands before shaping the pork balls so the mixture does not stick to your fingers. Use minced chicken instead of pork, if you prefer.

1   In a bowl, mix together the galangal, cilantro, shallots, minced pork, lime zest, and juice. Stir in the egg to bind the mixture together.

2   With damp hands, shape the mixture into 12 small balls around the lemon grass stalks, pressing the mixture firmly around each stalk. Chill for one hour to firm up.

3   Wrap the ends of the stalks with foil to prevent them burning under the grill. Brush the pork balls with peanut oil and grill for about 10 minutes, turning over occasionally, until cooked through. Sprinkle with the red chili pepper and serve with a dipping sauce.

SCALLOPS WITH LEMON GRASS BROTH & SPINACH

SERVES 4 • PREPARATION: 10 MINUTES • COOKING: 5 MINUTES.

1¼ cups chicken broth
1 tbsp lemon grass, sliced fine
4 scallions, chopped
½ red chili, seeded and chopped very fine
½ green bell pepper, seeded and chopped fine
4 oz enoki mushrooms
½ tsp granulated sugar
1 tbsp fish sauce
Juice of 1 lime
2 tbsp peanut oil
12 scallops without roes
3 oz baby spinach leaves

Scallops have very delicate flesh that quickly overcooks and becomes tough. Make sure the skillet is really hot, and sear the scallops quickly on each side so they are lightly golden on the outside but soft and succulent on the inside.

1   Put the broth, lemon grass, scallions, red chili, green bell pepper, enoki mushrooms, granulated sugar, fish sauce, and lime juice in a saucepan and simmer for five minutes.

2   Meanwhile, heat the peanut oil in a heavy skillet and when very hot, sear the scallops for about one minute on each side until just cooked.

3   Add the spinach to the broth and continue to simmer until the leaves have just wilted. Divide between serving dishes with the scallops served on top.

SWEET & AROMATIC SNAPPER

SERVES 4 • PREPARATION: 15 MINUTES • COOKING: 10 MINUTES

6 tbsp peanut oil
1 red onion, peeled and chopped fine
1 red bell pepper, seeded and chopped
1 tsp fresh ginger puree
2 garlic cloves, peeled and crushed
1 stalk of lemon grass, sliced very fine
3 medium tomatoes, peeled, seeded, and chopped
1 tbsp rice vinegar
2 tsp granulated sugar
½ cup water
1¼ lb red snapper fillets
4 tbsp all-purpose flour

The sauce also goes well with other fish fillets such as angler fish or tuna or it could be served spooned over grilled or fried chicken breasts.

1   Heat 2 tablespoons of peanut oil in a wok and fry the red onion over a medium heat for two minutes. Add the red bell pepper, fry for three minutes, then add the ginger, garlic, and lemon grass and fry for a further two minutes.

2   Add the tomatoes, rice vinegar, granulated sugar, and water and leave to simmer while you cook the fish.

3   Dust the snapper fillets with the flour. Heat the remaining peanut oil in a large skillet and fry the fish for two to three minutes on each side until golden brown and cooked through.

4   Serve the fish with boiled or stir-fried rice with the sauce spooned over.

RIGHT Scallops with lemon grass broth and spinach

CAMBODIA

MEKONG FISH CURRY

SERVES 4 • PREPARATION: 30 MINUTES • COOKING: 20 MINUTES

Curry paste:

3 garlic cloves, peeled and
   chopped
1 stalk of lemon grass,
   chopped or 1 tsp fresh
   lemon grass puree
1 red onion, peeled and
   chopped
1 tsp fresh ginger puree
1 tbsp coriander seeds
1 red chili, seeded and
   chopped
$1/2$ tsp ground turmeric
4 tbsp peanut oil

Fish curry:

9 oz zucchini, sliced
2 tbsp fish sauce
1 tbsp lime juice
1 tsp granulated brown
   sugar
1 tsp fresh lemon grass
   puree
12 fl oz coconut milk
1 lb firm white fish fillet,
   such as angler fish, cut
   into 1-in pieces
6 oz raw peeled shrimp

Cambodia's cuisine is very similar to the food of its Thai and Laotian neighbors with a hint of Chinese added to the mix. Rice is Cambodia's staple food and is served as an accompaniment to every meal, including a curry like this one.

1   To make the curry paste, place the garlic, lemon grass, red onion, ginger, coriander, red chili, turmeric, and half the peanut oil in a food processor and blend to a paste.

2   To cook the curry, heat the remaining peanut oil in a wok, add the curry paste, and cook over a gentle heat for 10 minutes, stirring occasionally.

3   Add the zucchini, fish sauce, lime juice, brown sugar, lemon grass puree, and coconut milk and simmer gently for five minutes.

4   Stir in the fish and shrimp and simmer for a further five minutes until they are cooked and the zucchini are tender. Serve with boiled or steamed rice.

THAILAND

HOT & SOUR CHICKEN SOUP

SERVES 4 · PREPARATION: 15 MINUTES · COOKING: 10 MINUTES

3 cups light but well-
flavored chicken broth

1 tsp fresh lemon grass
puree

1 tsp fresh ginger puree

2 kaffir lime leaves, cut into
wafer-thin slices

3 tbsp Thai fish sauce

4 tbsp lime juice

1 large red chili, seeded and
sliced thin

2 chicken breasts, skinned
and cut into small pieces

4 shiitake mushrooms,
sliced

8 snow peas, sliced
lengthwise

6 scallions, sliced thin

To garnish:

2 tbsp chopped fresh
cilantro leaves

Known in Thailand as *Tom Yum*, this popular soup, a fiery hot-sour mix of chiles, aromatic lemon grass, and lime leaves simmered in a well-flavored chicken broth. Chicken, mushrooms, vegetables, and shrimp can all be added to the basic mix but if you do not like things too hot, go easy on how much chile you put in.

1   Pour the broth into a large saucepan and bring to a boil. Add the lemon grass, ginger, and lime leaves and simmer for five minutes. Stir in the Thai fish sauce, lime juice, and red chili.

2   Add the chicken, shiitake mushrooms, snow peas, and scallions and simmer for five minutes.

3   Spoon into soup bowls and serve with the chopped cilantro sprinkled over.

VIETNAM

LEMON GRASS PORK ON PINEAPPLE

SERVES 4 · PREPARATION: 15 MINUTES · COOKING: 20 MINUTES

2 tbsp peanut oil
1 small onion, peeled and
    chopped fine
1 tsp finely sliced lemon
    grass
1 tsp chopped fine
    cilantro root
8 oz lean minced pork
1 tbsp fish sauce
2 tbsp light soy sauce
1 tbsp tomato ketchup
²/₃ cup chicken broth
1 tsp granulated sugar
2 oz unsalted peanuts,
    roasted and chopped fine
4 slices of pineapple

To garnish:
Cilantro leaves and chopped
    red chili

The tart flavor of the pineapple goes perfectly with the spiced pork topping, and the finely chopped chile gives it an added kick. The peanuts can be roasted in a heavy dry skillet or in a moderate oven spread out on a baking sheet.

1   Heat the peanut oil in a skillet, add the onion, and cook gently for three to four minutes until softened.

2   Add the lemon grass and cilantro root and cook for one minute, then stir in the pork, breaking up any lumps of meat with a spoon.

3   Fry until the pork is no longer pink, then add the fish sauce, light soy sauce, tomato ketchup, and chicken broth. Simmer over a low heat, stirring occasionally, for about 10 minutes until most of the liquid has evaporated. Add the sugar and allow to cool.

4   Stir half the peanuts into the pork mixture and spoon onto the pineapple slices to serve. Garnish with cilantro leaves, finely chopped red chili, and the remaining peanuts sprinkled over.

FISH SAUCES

Fish sauce is an indigenous ingredient in Thai, Vietnamese, Filipino, and Cambodian cuisines where it is known respectively as *nam pla*, *nuoc mam*, *patis*, and *nguoc mam*. Made from fermented fish or shrimp, fish sauce is rich in protein and B vitamins and is often used in much the same way as soy sauce in China. Shrimp paste, known across Southeast Asia as *terasi*, *trassie*, *balachan*, *kapi*, *ngapi*, and *blachen*, is a dense block of fermented ground shrimp paste ranging from pink to blackish-brown in color. Shrimp paste lasts indefinitely but should be cooked before eating. Use sparingly as it is very strong and extremely salty. Oyster sauce is a Chinese stir-fry sauce made from ground oysters, water, salt, cornstarch, and caramel. Bottles should be refrigerated after opening, and it's worth checking food labels to buy a brand that doesn't contain monosodium glutamate.

¹/₂ tsp fresh galangal puree
6 tbsp oyster sauce
1 tsp sweet chili sauce
1 tbsp dark soy sauce
1 tbsp rice vinegar
1 lb tuna, cut into
    2-in chunks

CHINA

TUNA GLAZED WITH CHILI & OYSTER SAUCE

SERVES 4 • MARINATING: 30 MINUTES • PREPARATION: 10 MINUTES
COOKING: 6–8 MINUTES

Most chefs will serve tuna very rare but if you prefer it well done, cook it for longer to your own personal preference. The cooking time given here is for medium rather than rare, because the marinade needs time to reduce to a sticky glaze over the fish.

1   In a bowl, mix together the galangal puree, oyster sauce, chili sauce, dark soy sauce, and rice vinegar. Add the tuna and stir until all the pieces are coated. Leave in a cool place to marinate for 30 minutes.

2   Transfer the tuna and marinade to a shallow pan and grill for six to eight minutes, turning over the chunks of fish halfway and basting with any juices in the pan. The tuna should be well glazed but not overcooked.

3   Serve with rice and stir-fried vegetables.

CHINA

STICKY RIBS

SERVES 4 · MARINATING: 8 HOURS · PREPARATION: 20 MINUTES
COOKING: 2 HOURS

1½ lb pork spare ribs
2 tbsp oyster sauce
4 tbsp rice wine
4 tbsp dark soy sauce
2 tbsp black bean
stir-fry sauce
⅔ cup fresh
orange juice

These will be a hit at any lunch or supper party served with finger bowls and plenty of paper napkins.

1   Spread out the spare ribs in a shallow dish. Mix together the oyster sauce, rice wine, dark soy sauce, and black bean sauce and spoon over the ribs until coated. Cover and leave in a cool place to marinate overnight.

2   Preheat the oven to 325°F. Transfer the ribs to a roasting tin with any marinade left in the dish. Pour over the orange juice, cover the tin with foil, and bake the ribs in the oven for 90 minutes.

3   Remove the foil, increase the oven temperature to 375°F, and cook the ribs for a further 30 minutes, basting them with the juices in the tin from time to time until the ribs are coated with a sticky glaze.

4   Serve hot as a starter for a Chinese meal, or as a main course with rice.

CHINA

STIR-FRIED SNOW PEAS WITH SHIITAKE MUSHROOMS

SERVES 4–6 · PREPARATION: 10 MINUTES · COOKING: 1¹/₂ MINUTES

A simple vegetable dish that's quick and easy to prepare and cook. It can be served as an accompaniment to meat or fish dishes or as part of a vegetarian meal.

2 tbsp peanut oil
12 oz snow peas, sliced lengthwise
5 oz shiitake mushrooms, sliced
2 tbsp oyster sauce
2 tbsp blanched almonds, lightly toasted and chopped fine

1   Heat the peanut oil in a wok and stir-fry the snow peas over a high heat for 30 seconds.

2   Add the shiitake mushrooms and stir-fry for one minute. Add the oyster sauce and toss together for a few seconds to heat through. Serve sprinkled with the chopped almonds.

THAILAND

CHICKEN PAD THAI

SERVES 4 · PREPARATION: 20 MINUTES · COOKING: 10 MINUTES

Chicken pad thai is one of Thailand's most popular dishes. This noodle mixture is sometimes served rolled up in a fine omelet net made by drizzling beaten egg over the inside of a hot wok with a birch whisk and cooking the egg until it sets in a thin lace net. The edge of the net is loosened with a palette knife and then carefully eased out of the wok.

2 tbsp chopped coarse cilantro leaves
1 medium red chili, seeded and chopped fine
¹/₂ cup peanut oil
12 oz medium flat rice noodles
9 oz chicken breasts, cut into ¹/₂-in pieces
4 pink shallots, peeled and chopped
1 tbsp granulated sugar
4 large eggs, beaten
1 tbsp oyster sauce
2 tbsp Thai fish sauce
Juice of 1 lime
9 oz beansprouts
4 scallions, sliced
4 oz unsalted, roasted peanuts, chopped

1   Mix together the chopped cilantro, chili, and peanut oil.

2   Cook the rice noodles according to the package instructions. Drain and set aside.

3   Pour the cilantro and chili oil into a wok and when hot, stir-fry the chicken and shallots for two minutes. Add the sugar and eggs and cook for a further one minute, stirring frequently to scramble the eggs as they start to set.

4   Stir in the oyster sauce, fish sauce, lime juice, and noodles. Stir-fry for two minutes, then add the beansprouts, scallions, and half the peanuts. Toss everything together over a fairly high heat until piping hot.

5   Tip onto serving plates and serve with the remaining peanuts on top.

RIGHT Stir-fried snow peas with shiitake mushrooms

THAILAND

CHICKEN, MANGO, & RICE SALAD

SERVES 4 · PREPARATION: 25 MINUTES (PLUS COOLING) · COOKING: 2 MINUTES

²/₃ cup water

1 tbsp Thai fish sauce

¹/₂ tsp shrimp paste

1 tbsp granulated brown sugar

1 tsp fresh lemon grass puree

Zest and juice of 1 lime, grated fine

1 tbsp Thai basil, torn fine

1 lb cold cooked rice

1 green mango, peeled, flesh cut away from the stone, and sliced thin

1 lb cooked chicken meat, sliced

4 oz beansprouts

4 oz green beans, cooked

1 slice of pineapple, cut into small pieces

1 green chili, sliced fine

Thai salads are hot and sour and use lots of fresh vegetables and herbs such as basil, chives, and mint. Instead of chicken, this recipe can also be made with mixed seafood such as scallops, squid, and shrimp.

1 Place the water in a saucepan with the Thai fish sauce, shrimp paste, granulated sugar, lemon grass puree, lime zest, and juice and bring to a boil. Simmer for two minutes, then remove from the heat and stir in the basil. Set aside to cool.

2 Divide the rice between four cups or small basins, pressing down so the rice is quite tightly packed, then turn out onto four serving plates.

3 Arrange the mango, chicken, beansprouts, green beans, and pineapple around the rice and scatter over the green chili. Spoon over a little of the dressing and serve the rest separately.

VIETNAM

PORK STIR-FRIED WITH GARLIC & FISH SAUCE

SERVES 4 · PREPARATION: 20 MINUTES · COOKING: 10 MINUTES

Juice of 1 lime
1 tsp fresh garlic puree
1 tbsp granulated
   brown sugar
2 red chilies, seeded and
   sliced fine
3 tbsp Thai fish sauce
1 tbsp rice vinegar
4 tbsp peanut oil
1 lb lean pork, cut into
   $^1/_2$-in pieces
1 red bell pepper, seeded
   and chopped
4 oz green beans, chopped
7 oz fine rice noodles,
   cooked according to the
   package instructions
2 tbsp chopped
   cilantro leaves
1 tbsp snipped fresh chives

Garlic, fish sauce, and lime juice are indigenous to most Thai stir-fry sauces but few cooks use formal recipes, preferring to taste as they progress and adjust the quantities of seasoning—and the number of chilies they add—to personal taste.

1   Mix together the lime juice, garlic, granulated sugar, red chilies, Thai fish sauce, and rice vinegar, stirring until the brown sugar dissolves.

2   Heat half the peanut oil in a wok and stir-fry the pork in two or three batches over a brisk heat for three to four minutes or until lightly browned. Remove from the wok and set aside.

3   Add the rest of the oil to the wok and stir-fry the red bell pepper and green beans over a medium heat for three minutes.

4   Return the pork to the wok, add the noodles and garlic, and fish sauce mixture, and toss over the heat for two to three minutes until everything is piping hot. Serve with the cilantro and chives sprinkled over.

KOREA

SQUID WITH TAMARIND SAUCE

SERVES 4 · PREPARATION: 20 MINUTES · COOKING: 7 MINUTES

²/₃ cup rice wine

1 tbsp tamarind paste

2 tbsp nuoc mam

1 tsp fresh lemon
grass puree

1 garlic clove, peeled
and crushed

1 tsp granulated
brown sugar

2 tbsp peanut oil

1 lb squid, cleaned and cut
into bite-size pieces

Flour, to dust

4 scallions, sliced

4 plum tomatoes, quartered

Nuoc mam, Vietnam's fish sauce, defines its country's cuisine more than any other ingredient. In this recipe it is combined with tamarind, the sour bean-shaped fruit of the tree of the same name. Tamarind paste is available ready to use in jars, or it can be bought in sticky blocks as a pulp. If you use the pulp, heat the rice wine until boiling and pour it over the pulp. Leave for 15 minutes to infuse, then strain before adding the remaining sauce ingredients.

1   Whisk together the rice wine, tamarind paste, nuoc mam, lemon grass, garlic, and brown sugar.

2   Heat the peanut oil in a wok. Dust the squid lightly with flour, add to the wok, and stir-fry over a brisk heat for three minutes or until lightly golden.

3   Add the scallions and tomatoes and stir-fry for two minutes. Pour in the sauce and toss the ingredients together until they are coated.

4   Simmer for two minutes until the sauce bubbles and reduces a little. Transfer to a serving dish and serve with rice and steamed vegetables.

VIETNAM

RICE PAPER ROLLS WITH NUOC CHAM

SERVES 4 · PREPARATION: 30 MINUTES · COOKING: 15 MINUTES

Rolls:
7 oz minced pork
4 oz raw jumbo shrimp,
    peeled and chopped fine
4 scallions, chopped fine
4 oz shiitake mushrooms,
    chopped fine
4 oz canned water
    chestnuts, chopped fine
1 small carrot, grated
1 tsp fresh ginger puree
1 tbsp nuoc mam
1 egg white, lightly frothed
8-in rice-paper or spring-
    roll wrappers
Peanut oil for deep-frying

Nuoc Cham:
1 tbsp granulated sugar
1 tbsp fresh lime juice
3 tbsp nuoc mam
3 tbsp rice vinegar
2 garlic cloves, peeled
    and crushed
1 red chili, seeded and
    sliced fine

More fine and delicate than Chinese spring-roll wrappers, Vietnamese rice-paper wrappers are available dried in pancakes and need soaking briefly in warm water to make them soft and pliable.

1   To make the rolls, in a bowl mix together the minced pork, jumbo shrimp, scallions, shiitake mushrooms, water chestnuts, carrot, ginger, and nuoc mam. Stir in about half the egg white until combined.

2   Dip the rice-paper wrappers briefly in warm water to soften them, lift out and place on a board. Put a spoonful of the filling in the center of the wrapper, brush the edges with a little of the remaining egg white, and roll up, tucking in the sides of the wrapper and pressing the brushed edges together to seal.

3   Repeat with the remaining filling and wrappers.

4   To make the nuoc cham, stir the granulated sugar into the lime juice, nuoc mam, and rice vinegar until dissolved and then stir in the garlic and chili.

5   Deep fry the rolls in batches in hot oil at 350°F for four to five minutes until golden. Drain on paper towels, and serve hot with the dip.

CHINA

CHINESE BRAISED SHRIMP & VEGETABLES IN OYSTER SAUCE

SERVES 4 · PREPARATION: 15 MINUTES · COOKING: 6 MINUTES

8 oz choy sum
2 tbsp peanut oil
1 red bell pepper, seeded and chopped
4 oz small mushrooms, such as shimeji
1 lb raw shrimp, peeled
1/2 cup chicken broth
1 tsp cornstarch
2 tbsp oyster sauce
1/2 tsp granulated sugar

Choy sum looks very similar to bok choy but the leaves have thin stalks, are lighter green in color, and sometimes have small yellow flowers that can be cooked along with the leaves.

1   Shred the choy sum leaves and chop the stalks, keeping the two separate.

2   Heat the peanut oil in a wok and stir-fry the red bell pepper, mushrooms, and choy sum stalks for three minutes. Remove from the wok and set aside.

3   Add the shrimp to the wok and stir-fry for one minute. Remove and set aside.

4   Mix a little of the chicken broth with the cornstarch until smooth, and add to the wok with the rest of the broth, the oyster sauce, and granulated sugar. Bring to a boil, stirring until smooth and thickened.

5   Return the vegetables and shrimp to the wok, add the choy sum leaves, and stir over the heat for one minute. Serve with boiled rice.

SHRIMP, PAPAYA, & PEANUT SALAD

SERVES 4 · PREPARATION: 15 MINUTES

¹/₂ iceberg lettuce, shredded

1 ripe papaya, peeled, seeded, and flesh sliced

1 lb jumbo shrimp, cooked and peeled

¹/₂ cucumber, sliced or cut into batons

1 large carrot, peeled and cut into fine sticks

3 oz canned water chestnuts, drained and sliced thin

1 stick of celery, sliced

Dressing:

4 tbsp sunflower oil

¹/₂ tsp sweet chili sauce

2 tsp Thai fish sauce

2 tbsp crunchy peanut butter

1 garlic clove, peeled and crushed

Juice of 1 lime

To garnish:

2 oz unsalted peanuts, lightly toasted

Choose a ripe papaya rather than an under-ripe green one to give the salad a sweet, aromatic fragrance. You can buy ready-cooked shrimp, or stir-fry raw shrimp in a little hot oil with the juice of half a lime squeezed over.

1   Line a serving platter with the shredded lettuce and arrange the papaya slices, shrimp, cucumber batons, carrot sticks, sliced water chestnuts, and celery on top.

2   Whisk the ingredients for the dressing together until evenly combined, and spoon over the salad. Scatter the peanuts over and serve.

THAILAND

MUSSEL & SHRIMP FRITTERS

SERVES 4 • PREPARATION: 20 MINUTES (PLUS STANDING) • COOKING: 15 MINUTES

Fritters:
1 cup all-purpose flour,
  plus extra to dust
¹/₂ tsp baking powder
1 cup light beer
12 large mussels, such
  as greenlip
12 large raw shrimp, peeled
Peanut oil for deep-frying

Dip:
2 tbsp Thai fish sauce
2 tbsp lime juice
¹/₂ tsp sweet chili sauce
1 tsp granulated sugar

A popular street food in Bangkok, these fritters can be bought from road-side vendors who cook them fresh for customers. Use large mussels such as greenlip, and be sure to heat the oil to the correct temperature before you fry.

1   To make the fritters, sift the all-purpose flour and the baking powder into a mixing bowl. Make a well in the center, pour in half the beer, and stir until mixed well. Gradually whisk in the rest of the beer to make a smooth batter. Set aside to stand for one hour.

2   Dust the mussels and shrimp lightly in flour, and heat oil to 350°F for deep-frying.

3   To make the dip, stir the ingredients together in a small bowl until the granulated sugar dissolves.

4   Add a few mussels and shrimp to the batter, lift them out with tongs or a fork, and allow the excess batter to run back into the bowl. Add them to the hot oil and deep-fry for two to three minutes or until they are golden and crisp.

5   Drain the mussels and shrimp on a paper towel and fry the rest in batches in the same way. Serve the fritters hot with the dip.

廣西漲水
因爲黔水東調，沿途不少城市
都貼出安全通告，告誡各地居民在
調水期間不要在江邊逗留，以確保
安全。據介紹，調水期江上將會出
現「小洪峰」，江水會有不同程度
上漲。其中，最高漲幅將於 1 月 26
日、27 日左右出現在廣西來賓等
遊、沿江涉水工程建設的專項檢查，杜絕安全事故的發
須確保電網安全運行

CHINA

PEPPERED SHRIMP WITH GARLIC & CILANTRO

SERVES 4 · PREPARATION: 15 MINUTES · COOKING: 3 MINUTES

Szechuan peppercorns are round, reddish-brown berries with an aromatic fragrance and flavor. Used in Chinese Szechuan cuisine, which is more hot and spicy than Cantonese, this pepper is also found in Japan where it is sold ground, and known as *sansho*.

2 tbsp peanut oil

3 garlic cloves, peeled and chopped fine

1 tbsp finely chopped cilantro root

2 tsp Szechuan peppercorns, crushed coarse

1 lb raw jumbo shrimp, heads removed, halved lengthwise, and deveined

1 tbsp fish sauce

1 tsp granulated sugar

2 tbsp chopped cilantro leaf

1　Heat the peanut oil in a wok, add the garlic, cilantro root, and crushed Szechuan peppercorns and stir-fry over a medium heat for one minute.

2　Add the shrimp and cook for one to two minutes until they turn pink. Mix the fish sauce with the granulated sugar and chopped cilantro leaf, and drizzle over the shrimp.

SESAME

Used mainly in Japanese, Chinese, and Korean dishes, sesame is available as an oil, paste, or as black and white seeds. Ordinary sesame oil adds a distinct nutty flavor to dishes but toasted sesame oil should be used sparingly because it has a pungent flavor and can overwhelm other ingredients. Toasted sesame oil is usually drizzled over stir-fries to flavor them at the end of cooking, rather than being used for frying. When toasting sesame seeds, spread them in a heavy, dry skillet and place over a medium heat, but watch them carefully because they will quickly scorch.

4 chicken breasts
3 tbsp honey
1 tsp ginger puree
2 tbsp dark soy sauce
2 tbsp lime juice
2 tbsp peanut oil
8 scallions, sliced
1 red bell pepper, seeded and sliced
4 oz baby corn, chopped
3 oz shiitake mushrooms, quartered
1 tsp toasted sesame oil
2 oz unsalted cashews, lightly toasted
1 tsp black sesame seeds

CHINA

SESAME CHICKEN WITH CASHEWS

SERVES 4 • MARINATING: 4 HOURS • PREPARATION: 20 MINUTES • COOKING: 35 MINUTES

Shiitake mushrooms are available fresh from supermarkets or dried in bags from Asian stores. When using dried mushrooms, place them in a heatproof bowl and pour over boiling water to cover. Leave the mushrooms to stand for two to three hours before using—the soaking liquid can be used as a broth, but strain it first as it may be gritty.

1   Preheat the oven to 375°F.

2   Place the chicken breasts in a dish in a single layer. Mix together the honey, ginger puree, dark soy sauce, and lime juice. Pour over the chicken and set aside in a cool place to marinate for four hours, turning the chicken breasts over occasionally.

3   Transfer the chicken to a shallow ovenproof dish and reserve the marinade.

4   Cook the chicken in the oven for 25 minutes, basting occasionally with any juices in the dish.

5   When the chicken is almost ready, heat the peanut oil in a wok and stir-fry the scallions, red bell pepper, baby corn, and shiitake mushrooms for five minutes over a medium heat. Pour the reserved marinade over the vegetables, add two tablespoons of water and the sesame oil, and toss over the heat for one minute until the vegetables are coated in the sauce.

6   Divide the vegetables between serving plates. Cut the chicken into slices and scatter with the cashews and black sesame seeds.

CHINA

SOFT SHELL CRABS WITH SESAME-DRESSED VEGETABLES

SERVES 4 (AS A STARTER) • PREPARATION: 15 MINUTES • COOKING: 4–5 MINUTES

Crabs:
4 soft shell crabs
2 tbsp cornstarch
Peanut oil for
** deep-frying**

Salad:
¹/₂ cucumber, grated
3-in piece of white radish,
** grated**
1 large carrot, grated
2 tsp sesame oil
2 tsp mixed white and
** black sesame seeds**

Soft shell crabs are young freshwater crabs that are caught when they have shed their old shells and the replacement one has yet to harden. Fresh ones are available during the fall, frozen ones can be bought all year round.

1   Dust the crabs with cornstarch until well coated.

2   Heat the peanut oil to 350°F for deep-frying, and deep-fry the crabs for four to five minutes or until pink and crisp. Drain on a paper towel.

3   To make the salad, mix the cucumber, radish, and carrot together and toss with the sesame oil.

4   Divide the salad between serving plates, sit the crabs on top, and sprinkle over the white and black sesame seeds. Serve at once.

GREEN BEANS, CARROTS, & WHITE RADISH WITH TOFU DRESSING

SERVES 4 • PREPARATION: 10 MINUTES • COOKING: 2 MINUTES

7 oz green beans
1 large carrot, cut into sticks
3 oz white radish, peeled
  and cut into sticks

Dressing:
9 oz silken tofu
2 tbsp sesame seed
  paste (tahini)
2 tbsp light soy sauce
1 tsp superfine sugar
Juice of 1 lime
1 tbsp mixed black and
  white sesame seeds

A crisp crunchy salad with a creamy dressing that can be served on its own as a light lunch or supper dish, or as part of a Chinese meal.

1 Blanch the green beans, carrot, and white radish in a pan of boiling water for two minutes. Drain and cool by running cold water through the sieve.

2 To make the dressing, puree the silken tofu in a food processor with the sesame seed paste, soy sauce, superfine sugar, and lime juice. If the dressing is too thick, stir in enough cold water to bring it to the desired consistency.

3 Spread out the vegetables on a serving dish and spoon over the dressing. Sprinkle with the black and white sesame seeds and serve.

JAPAN

ORIENTAL SALMON SALAD

SERVES 4 • MARINATING: 1 HOUR • PREPARATION: 15 MINUTES • COOKING: 5 MINUTES

1 lb salmon fillet, skinned
  and cut into strips
3 tbsp light soy sauce
2 tbsp sesame oil
1 tsp granulated
  brown sugar
2 tbsp rice vinegar
1 tbsp peanut oil
1 stick of celery, sliced
1 yellow bell pepper, seeded
  and sliced
3 scallions, sliced
¼ cucumber, cut into sticks
2 radishes, sliced

Cook the salmon briefly over a fairly high heat so a golden-brown crust forms on the outside but the center is still sweet and juicy.

1 Place the salmon in a shallow dish. Mix together the light soy sauce, sesame oil, granulated brown sugar, and rice vinegar and pour over the fish. Cover and leave in a cool place to marinate for one hour.

2 Heat the peanut oil in a wok, drain the salmon from the marinade, and fry quickly over a brisk heat for one minute or until the pieces are browned. Remove the salmon and set aside.

3 Add the celery, yellow bell pepper, and scallions to the wok and stir-fry for three to four minutes until they start to soften. Add the cucumber, radishes, and the marinade left in the dish and toss over the heat for one minute.

4 Divide the vegetables between plates and lay the salmon pieces on top.

RIGHT Green beans, carrots, and white radish with tofu dressing

CHINA

SESAME & GINGER SEA BASS

SERVES 4 · PREPARATION: 15 MINUTES · COOKING: 15 MINUTES

Four 6-oz sea bass fillets, skin on
8 scallions, sliced into thin strips
1 small knob of gingerroot, peeled and sliced very thin
3 tbsp light soy sauce
1 tbsp fish sauce
1 tbsp rice vinegar
2 tbsp sesame oil
2 tbsp white sesame seeds

A light, aromatic fish dish that's quick and easy to prepare. Serve the fish with snow peas stir-fried with beansprouts and button mushrooms.

1 Preheat the oven to 400°F.

2 Cut four squares of foil, each one large enough to enclose a sea bass fillet.

3 Place one fish fillet, skin side down, on each square of foil, and top with the scallions and ginger. Mix together the soy sauce, fish sauce, and rice vinegar and spoon over the fish.

4 Drizzle the sea bass with the sesame oil and wrap the foil, around the fish, folding over the edges to make tightly sealed parcels. Place the parcels on a baking sheet and cook in the oven for 15 minutes.

5 Unwrap the parcels and sprinkle the fish with white sesame seeds before serving.

CHINA

STIR-FRIED LAMB WITH SESAME NOODLES

SERVES 4 • MARINATING: 4 HOURS • PREPARATION: 15 MINUTES • COOKING: 20 MINUTES

12 oz lean lamb, cut into strips
4 tbsp dark soy sauce
2 tbsp hoi sin sauce
2 tsp honey
1 tsp fresh ginger puree
3 tbsp peanut oil
1 red bell pepper, seeded and sliced
4 oz beansprouts
2 heads of bok choy, shredded
11 oz fresh egg noodles
1 tsp toasted sesame oil
2 tbsp white sesame seeds

The lamb can be prepared the day before needed, if preferred, and left to marinate overnight.

1 Place the lamb in a shallow dish. Mix together the dark soy sauce, hoi sin sauce, honey, and ginger and pour over the lamb. Cover and leave in a cool place to marinate for four hours or longer.

2 Heat 1 tablespoon of peanut oil in a wok and stir-fry the red bell pepper over a medium heat for three to four minutes until starting to soften. Add the beansprouts and bok choy and stir-fry for a further four minutes. Remove the vegetables from the wok and set aside.

3 Add the remaining peanut oil to the wok and turn up the heat to high. Drain the lamb from the marinade, add to the wok, and stir-fry for three to four minutes. Add the egg noodles and vegetables and pour over any marinade left in the dish.

4 Toss everything together over the heat for about five minutes until hot. Drizzle with the sesame oil, sprinkle with sesame seeds, and serve at once.

KOREAN GREEN BEAN & SCALLION PANCAKES

SERVES 4 · PREPARATION: 1 HOUR (PLUS STANDING) · COOKING: 25 MINUTES

Dipping sauce 1:
4 tbsp Japanese soy sauce
1 tbsp rice vinegar
$^1/_2$ tsp fresh ginger puree
1 tsp sesame seed
  paste (tahini)
Pinch of granulated sugar
1 tsp black sesame seeds

Dipping sauce 2:
4 tbsp light soy sauce
1 tsp white sesame seeds

Pancakes:
2 oz green beans
3 oz all-purpose flour
3 oz rice flour
1 large egg, beaten
1 cup cold water
1 tsp toasted sesame oil
2 tbsp peanut oil
4 scallions, sliced into
  thin strips
$^1/_2$ red bell pepper, cut
  into thin strips

These small pancakes make popular street food in Korea where they are known locally as "pizza." Confusing to Europeans who compare them with the Italian version—but delicious just the same.

1 To make the first dipping sauce, mix together the Japanese soy sauce and rice vinegar and stir in the other ingredients. To make the second dipping sauce, put the soy sauce in a bowl and sprinkle over the white sesame seeds.

2 To make the pancakes, blanch the green beans in a saucepan of boiling water for one minute. Drain, cool under cold water, and chop into small pieces.

3 In a bowl, mix together the all-purpose flour and rice flour. Make a well in the center, add the egg, and stir into the flours until mixed, gradually adding the cold water. When you have a smooth batter, stir in the sesame oil and leave to stand for 30 minutes. Pour the batter into a jug.

4 Heat 1 tablespoon of peanut oil in a small, heavy, non-stick skillet about 7 ins in diameter and pour in a quarter of the batter. Add a quarter of the beans, scallions, and red bell pepper and cook over a medium heat for three to four minutes until the pancake is set and browned underneath.

5 Flip the pancake over and cook for a further two to three minutes. Remove it from the skillet to a plate and keep warm. Make three more pancakes with the remaining ingredients, adding more oil to the skillet as necessary.

6 Serve the pancakes hot, cut into squares with the dipping sauces.

CHINA

SESAME STEAMED SHRIMP WITH STAR ANISE

SERVES 4-6 • PREPARATION: 10 MINUTES • COOKING: 10 MINUTES

1 lb raw shrimp
2 tbsp dark soy sauce
1 tbsp rice wine
1 tsp honey
$^1/_2$ tsp toasted sesame oil
2 whole star anise
Small knob of gingerroot,
   peeled and shredded
1 tbsp white sesame seeds

Star anise is a popular spice in Chinese cuisine and has a sweet liquorice-like flavor. The fruit of a tree from the magnolia family that can grow to a height of 45 feet, each one is a perfect mahogany-brown eight-point star containing a tiny seed in each point.

1   Peel and devein the shrimp, leaving the tails on. Spread out on a heat-proof plate.

2   Mix together the dark soy sauce, rice wine, honey, and sesame oil and brush over the shrimp. Tuck the star anise among the shrimp and scatter over the ginger and sesame seeds.

3   Steam for 10 minutes, or until the shrimp turn pink. Serve with stir-fried mixed vegetables.

CHINA

BLACK SESAME CRISPS

MAKES 20 • PREPARATION: 10 MINUTES • COOKING: 3 MINUTES

5 spring-roll wrappers,
   about 8 in square
1 egg white, beaten
2 tbsp black sesame seeds
Peanut oil for
   deep-frying
Salt

Don't add too many crisps to the frying basket at any one time or they will lower the temperature of the oil and stick together, making the crisps heavy and chewy rather than light and crisp.

1   Cut each spring-roll wrapper into four squares and brush with beaten egg white. Scatter over the black sesame seeds.

2   Heat the peanut oil to 350°F for deep-frying, and fry the crisps three or four at a time for 30 to 40 seconds until golden brown and crisp.

3   Drain on a paper towel and sprinkle lightly with salt. Serve on their own or with a sweet chili dipping sauce (*see* page 45).

LEFT Black sesame crisps

CHINA

BON-BON CHICKEN

SERVES 4 · PREPARATION: 15 MINUTES

4 oz crunchy
  peanut butter
1 tsp sweet chili sauce
2 tbsp dark soy sauce
²/₃ cup coconut milk
5 tbsp sunflower oil
1 tsp toasted sesame oil
Juice of 2 limes
1 bag of mixed salad leaves
2 carrots, cut into sticks
4 scallions, sliced thin
1 lb cooked chicken meat,
  shredded

To garnish:
Lime wedges
Black and white
  sesame seeds

In the West this dish has come to be called "Bang Bang Chicken," but in China it is known as "Bon-Bon Chicken" after the stick (*bon*) used to bash and tenderize the meat.

1 Place the peanut butter, chili sauce, dark soy sauce, and coconut milk in a food processor and blend together. With the motor running, drizzle the sunflower oil down the feeder tube. When all the oil has been incorporated into the mix, add the sesame oil and lime juice.

2 Divide the salad leaves, carrots, and scallions between serving plates and pile the chicken on top.

3 The peanut sauce should be thick enough to coat the chicken, but if it is too thick, thin it with a little warm water before spooning over.

4 Serve garnished with lime wedges and the black and white sesame seeds sprinkled over.

CHINESE TOFFEE BANANAS

SERVES 4 • PREPARATION: 10 MINUTES (PLUS STANDING) • COOKING: 25 MINUTES

Batter:

4 oz all-purpose flour, plus extra for dusting

About ¹/₂ cup cold water

2 tsp peanut oil, plus extra for deep-frying

Toffee bananas:

4 medium, under-ripe bananas, peeled and cut into 2-in lengths

1 tsp sesame oil

12 oz superfine sugar

³/₄ cup water

3 tbsp white sesame seeds

When making the caramel, don't let the syrup boil until all the sugar dissolves or it will have a granular texture. As the syrup heats up, brush down any stray sugar crystals sticking to the sides of the pan.

1 Sift the flour into a bowl and stir in enough cold water to make a smooth batter. Stir in two teaspoons of peanut oil and set aside for 30 minutes.

2 Dust the banana pieces in all-purpose flour.

3 Heat the peanut oil to 375°F for deep-frying. Drop six pieces of banana into the batter, lift out one at a time with a fork or slotted spoon, and lower into the hot peanut oil.

4 Fry in three or four batches for two to three minutes until golden and then drain on a paper towel. Fry all the banana pieces in the same way.

5 Grease a large plate with the sesame oil and prepare a bowl filled with cold water and ice cubes.

6 Put the superfine sugar in a large saucepan or wok and pour in the water. Heat gently, stirring until the sugar dissolves, and then increase the heat and boil rapidly until the syrup caramelizes to a rich golden brown.

7 Remove the pan from the heat, add the sesame seeds and bananas, and stir until coated. Immediately tip out the banana pieces onto the plate and with two forks or chopsticks, pick up the pieces one at a time and dip them in the iced water to harden the toffee. Serve while still warm.

4 oz white sesame seeds
6 oz unsalted peanuts,
    coarsely chopped
2 oz blanched almonds,
    coarsely chopped
2 cups superfine sugar
1$^{1}/_{2}$ cups granulated brown
    sugar
$^{3}/_{4}$ cup corn syrup
$^{2}/_{3}$ cup water
Pinch of baking soda

CHINA

SESAME NUT BRITTLE

MAKES ABOUT 900 G / 2 LB · PREPARATION: 30 MINUTES · COOKING: 15 MINUTES

Desserts are not as popular in Asia as they are in the West but this sweet, toffee-like treat makes a good finale to a Chinese meal served with a pot of jasmine or green tea.

1 Preheat oven to 350°F.

2 Grease an 8-inch baking tin and line the base with non-stick baking parchment.

3 Spread out the sesame seeds, peanuts, and almonds on a baking sheet and toast in a the oven for four to five minutes or until lightly golden.

4 Place the sugars, corn syrup, and water in a pan and heat gently until the sugars dissolve. Bring to a boil and simmer until the corn syrup reaches 300°F (hard crack stage) on a sugar thermometer.

5 Add the baking soda, sesame seeds, peanuts, and almonds and pour slowly into the tin. Mark into bars when almost set, and cut when cold.

ASIAN HERBS & LEAVES

Asian food stores and market stalls sell a wide selection of indigenous herbs, salad greens, and leaves. These include bok choy, a small cabbage with white stalks and green leaves, which are excellent for stir-frying, *kai larn* ('Chinese broccoli'), and *ong choi* ('water spinach'). Basil is a popular herb in Thailand but the local variety, known as "holy basil" or *bai jorapa*, has a distinctive flavor of aniseed and small, deep green, oval-shaped leaves with purple stems and flowers, in contrast to its sweeter Mediterranean relative. Cilantro is probably Southeast Asia's most widely used herb, with both the leaves and chopped stems being added to dishes.

CHINA

CILANTRO & SHRIMP TOAST

MAKES 12 • PREPARATION: 15 MINUTES • COOKING: 4 MINUTES

12 raw jumbo shrimp,
    peeled but tails left on
2 eggs, beaten
2 tbsp cornstarch, plus extra
    for dusting
2 tbsp finely chopped
    cilantro leaf
1 tbsp snipped chives
6 small slices of white
    bread, crusts removed
Peanut oil for deep-frying

Press the shrimp down gently onto the bread slices so they do not fall off when they are dropped into the hot oil. As they fry, the tails will curl attractively away from the bread.

1   Cut each shrimp down the back without cutting all the way through and pull out the dark thread running the length of the shrimp. Open out each shrimp and flatten gently.

2   Beat together the eggs and cornstarch until smooth, then beat in the chopped cilantro and chives. Dust the shrimp with cornstarch.

3   Cut each slice of bread in half down the center. Dip the bread in the egg mixture, letting the excess drain off. Dip the shrimp in the egg mixture and place a shrimp, cut side down, on each piece of bread, pressing them down gently.

4   Heat peanut oil for deep-frying to 350°F and fry the shrimp toasts in three or four batches for about one minute until golden brown. Drain on a paper towel and serve hot with a sweet chili dipping sauce.

THAILAND

MINI VEGETABLE & HERB ROLLS

SERVES 4 · PREPARATION: 30 MINUTES · COOKING: 15 MINUTES

Do not pack the filling too tightly into the rolls or they will burst open when plunged into the hot oil.

2 tbsp peanut oil plus extra
    for deep-frying
3 oz grated carrot
3 oz Chinese cabbage,
    shredded fine
2 sticks of celery,
    diced fine
2 oz shiitake mushrooms,
    chopped fine
1 garlic clove, peeled
    and crushed
1 tbsp finely chopped
    celery leaves
1 tbsp snipped chives
1 tbsp chopped
    fresh parsley
5-in spring-roll wrappers
1 egg white, lightly beaten

To serve:
Dipping sauce, such as
    sweet and sour

1   Heat 2 tablespoons of peanut oil in a wok and stir-fry the carrot, Chinese cabbage, celery, shiitake mushrooms, and garlic for two to three minutes over a medium heat until just softened.

2   Stir in the celery leaves, chives, and parsley and set aside to cool.

3   Lay the spring-roll wrappers on a board and spoon a little of the filling onto each. Brush the edges of the wrappers with egg white and roll up from one corner to the opposite one, tucking in the sides and pressing the edges together to seal.

4   Heat the peanut oil to 350°F for deep-frying and fry the rolls in batches for about three minutes until golden brown. Drain on a paper towel and serve hot with a dipping sauce such as sweet and sour.

CHINA

CRISPY FRIED CHINESE GREENS WITH CASHEWS

SERVES 4 · PREPARATION: 10 MINUTES · COOKING: 2–3 MINUTES

2 garlic cloves
10 oz green leaves, such
 as bok choy, spinach,
 or green cabbage
Peanut oil for
 deep-frying
1 tsp salt
1 tsp granulated sugar
3 tbsp roasted cashews,
 chopped coarse

Dry the rinsed leaves thoroughly before you fry them as any remaining moisture will make the oil spit.

1 Peel the garlic and cut the cloves into very thin slices. Remove any tough stalks from the leaves and rinse them in cold water. Drain and dry thoroughly with a paper towel or a clean dish towel.

2 Roll up the leaves tightly, a couple at a time, and shred fine with a sharp knife.

3 Heat the peanut oil for deep-frying to 350°F and deep-fry the leaves, a handful at a time, for about 30 seconds until they become dark green and crisp. Drain each batch on a paper towel before adding the next batch to the fryer.

4 Fry the garlic slices with the last batch of greens, and then drain and toss with the rest. Sprinkle the greens with salt and sugar and scatter over the chopped cashews.

5 Serve as an accompaniment to a main course of stir-fried fish or meat, or as part of a selection of starters.

THAI BEEF & ARUGULA SALAD

SERVES 4 · PREPARATION: 15 MINUTES (PLUS CHILLING) · COOKING: 10 MINUTES

¹/₂ tsp chili powder
1 tsp ground coriander
¹/₂ tsp ground black pepper
Pinch of ground ginger
1 lb fillet mignon in
   one piece
1 tbsp peanut oil
¹/₂ tsp lemon grass puree
1 tbsp cilantro leaf,
   chopped rough
1 tbsp chopped mint leaves
1 tbsp fish sauce
2 tbsp rice vinegar
1 tsp superfine sugar
1 red chili, seeded and
   chopped fine
4 oz arugula leaves
1 oz red chard leaves
2 tbsp chopped cashews,
   lightly toasted
2 scallions, shredded

Add extra chili powder if you like a spicy dish but only add half if you prefer your salads to be cool.

1   Mix together the chili powder, coriander, black pepper, and ginger. Roll the fillet in the spice mix until coated.

2   Heat the peanut oil in a heavy skillet and seal the fillet on all sides until well browned. Allow to cool, then wrap tightly in plastic wrap and place in the freezer for 30 minutes.

3   Remove the fillet from the freezer, unwrap, and slice as thinly as possible.

4   Mix together the lemon grass, cilantro, mint, fish sauce, rice vinegar, superfine sugar, and red chili.

5   Arrange the fillet slices on the serving dish so that they overlap. Pile the arugula and chard leaves in the center and spoon over the dressing. Scatter over the cashews, and serve garnished with the scallions.

PORK CHOP SUEY

SERVES 4 · PREPARATION: 20 MINUTES · COOKING: 11–12 MINUTES

4 oz dried medium
    egg noodles
2 tbsp peanut oil
7 oz lean pork, cut into
    small pieces
2 carrots, cut into small dice
4 scallions, chopped
$1/2$ small red bell pepper,
    seeded and sliced
1 zucchini, sliced
1 tsp fresh ginger puree
12 oz Chinese leaves,
    shredded fine
4 oz beansprouts
3 tbsp light soy sauce
4 tbsp rice wine

Small peeled shrimp can replace the pork, or use finely chopped cooked ham.

1   Cook the noodles according to the instructions on the package and drain.

2   Heat one tablespoon of peanut oil in a wok and stir-fry the pork for two minutes over a high heat until browned. Remove from the wok and set aside.

3   Lower the heat to medium, add the rest of the peanut oil to the wok, and stir-fry the carrots for two minutes. Add the scallions, red bell pepper, and zucchini and stir-fry for three minutes.

4   Add the ginger, Chinese leaves, and beansprouts and stir-fry for two minutes. Return the pork to the wok, add the noodles, light soy sauce, and rice wine and toss together over the heat for two to three minutes until piping hot.

SINGAPORE

ASIAN MUSHROOM
& CHOY SUM BROTH

SERVES 4–6 · PREPARATION: 15 MINUTES · COOKING: 16 MINUTES

1 tsp fresh ginger puree
1 red shallot, peeled and
    chopped fine
1 garlic clove, peeled and
    chopped fine
2 tsp peanut oil
1 tsp granulated sugar
9 oz shiitake mushrooms,
    sliced
4 cups chicken or
    vegetable broth
2 tbsp dark soy sauce
4 heads of choy sum, sliced
3 oz enoki mushrooms,
    trimmed
2 oz edamame beans,
    removed from their pods

Other mushrooms such as brown cap or oyster can be used, depending on what is available. If cooking for vegetarians, use vegetable broth rather than chicken.

1   In a large saucepan or wok, fry the ginger, shallot, and garlic in the peanut oil over a gentle heat until soft. Add the sugar, stir over the heat for one minute, then add the shiitake mushrooms and pour in the broth and dark soy sauce.

2   Simmer for 10 minutes, add the choy sum, enoki mushrooms, and edamame beans, and simmer for a further five minutes.

3   Divide between serving bowls and serve at once.

VIETNAM

CILANTRO SHRIMP WITH MINT SAUCE

SERVES 4 • MARINATING: 2 HOURS • PREPARATION: 15 MINUTES • COOKING: 1–2 MINUTES

Large bunch of cilantro leaf, roots and coarse stalks discarded
2 garlic cloves, peeled and chopped rough
1 tsp fresh ginger puree
3 tbsp peanut oil
1 lb large raw shrimp, peeled with tails left on

Sauce:
²/₃ cup coconut milk
1 green chili, seeded and chopped fine
2 tbsp mint leaves, chopped fine
1 tsp black sesame seeds

Serve the shrimp straight from the wok with the sauce on the side. This dish makes a good light starter or appetizer.

1 Place the cilantro, garlic, ginger and two tablespoons of peanut oil in a blender and reduce to a smooth puree.

2 Spread out the shrimp in a shallow dish, coat with the cilantro puree, cover and leave in a cool place to marinate for two hours.

3 For the sauce, mix together the coconut milk, chili, and mint. Spoon into a small bowl and sprinkle over the black sesame seeds. Cover and chill until ready to serve.

4 Heat the remaining peanut oil in a wok and stir-fry the shrimp for one to two minutes until they turn pink. Pour in any marinade left in the dish and allow to simmer briefly. Serve the shrimp with the sauce.

JAPAN

STEAMED SEA BASS WITH ASIAN GREENS

SERVES 2 • PREPARATION: 15 MINUTES • COOKING: 6–7 MINUTES

Steaming is an excellent way to cook fish as its flesh stays moist and is less likely to dry out.

Two 5-oz sea bass fillets
Salt and pepper
2 heads of baby bok choy, halved
4 sprigs of Chinese broccoli
2 oz water spinach
1 small knob of gingerroot, peeled and cut into fine shreds
1 tsp sesame oil
4 tbsp rice wine
2 tbsp light soy sauce

1 Cut each sea bass fillet in half and season with salt and pepper.

2 Place the bok choy, Chinese broccoli, and water spinach on a plate with the sea bass on top. Add the ginger and drizzle over the sesame oil, rice wine, and light soy sauce.

3 Place the plate in a steamer, cover and steam for six to seven minutes or until the fish is cooked and the greens are just tender.

CHINA

STEAMED ORIENTAL FISH

SERVES 4 • MARINATING: 3–4 HOURS • PREPARATION: 15 MINUTES
COOKING: 40 MINUTES

3–4 lb whole fish, such as carp, snapper, sea bream, cleaned
1 in gingerroot, peeled and shredded fine
2 garlic cloves, peeled and sliced thin
1 tbsp sesame oil
2 tbsp rice vinegar
5 tbsp light soy sauce
2 tsp granulated brown sugar
4 slices of lotus root, halved if large
4 water chestnuts, sliced
1 carrot, cut into sticks
2 scallions, shredded
7 oz Chinese broccoli
8 heads of flowering chives, trimmed

One large fish makes an impressive main course for a dinner party, but four small fish or fish steaks will work equally well. If using small fish, the steaming time needs to be halved.

1 Place the fish in a large dish and sprinkle over the ginger and garlic, tucking some inside the fish. Mix together the sesame oil, rice vinegar, light soy sauce, and sugar and pour over the fish. Set aside to marinate for three to four hours.

2 Lift the fish onto a steaming rack for a wok or large bamboo steamer, bending it round if it is too large to fit on the rack.

3 Fill the wok one-third with water and sit the fish on the rack inside. Tuck the lotus root, water chestnuts, and carrot over and around the fish. Cover and steam for 30 minutes. Add the scallions, broccoli, and chives and simmer for a further 10 minutes or until the flesh of the fish flakes easily.

LEFT Steamed oriental fish

2 tbsp Thai fish sauce

2 tbsp dark soy sauce

$^1/_2$ tsp granulated sugar

2 tbsp peanut oil

4 red shallots, peeled
and sliced

$^1/_2$ yellow bell pepper,
seeded and chopped

2 garlic cloves, peeled
and chopped

1 red chili, seeded and
chopped fine

16 to 20 small (queen)
scallops

2 tbsp coarsely chopped
Thai basil

2 tbsp coarsely chopped
cilantro leaves

THAILAND

SCALLOPS WITH THAI BASIL, CILANTRO, & GARLIC

SERVES 2 • PREPARATION: 15 MINUTES • COOKING: 7 MINUTES

If you can't find Thai basil, substitute garlic chives. Mediterranean sweet basil could be used, but it will give the dish a different flavor.

1 Mix together the fish sauce, dark soy sauce, and sugar until the sugar dissolves.

2 Heat half the peanut oil in a skillet and fry the shallots and yellow bell pepper over a medium heat for three minutes. Add the garlic and red chili and fry for a further two to three minutes until the vegetables are just tender. Remove from the skillet and set aside.

3 Increase the heat under the skillet, add the remaining oil, and when very hot, sear the scallops on each side until lightly browned.

4 Pour the fish sauce mixture over the scallops and stir until they are coated. Return the vegetables to the skillet, add the basil and cilantro, and cook for one minute.

5 Serve hot with boiled or steamed rice or plain noodles.

JAPAN

CHILI VEGETABLE STIR-FRY

SERVES 4 • PREPARATION: 20 MINUTES • COOKING: 8 MINUTES

When buying choy sum, look for firm thin stalks and fresh green leaves with no brown spots. Use choy sum as soon as possible after buying because it does not store well. If choy sum is not available, bok choy could be used, but cut away any tough stalks before shredding the leaves.

2 tbsp peanut oil

3 oz unsalted
cashew nuts

9 oz firm tofu, cubed

1 red onion, peeled and
sliced fine

1 red bell pepper, seeded
and sliced thin

4 oz baby corn, chopped

4 shiitake mushrooms,
sliced

6 oz choy sum leaves,
shredded coarse

1 tsp chili sauce

2 tbsp light soy sauce

1 tbsp oyster sauce

1 tsp cornstarch

³/₄ cup vegetable broth

1   Heat the peanut oil in a wok and stir-fry the cashews for 30 seconds or until just golden. Drain the cashew nuts and set aside.

2   Add the tofu to the wok and fry lightly until golden. Remove and set aside. Add the onion and stir-fry for two minutes, then add the red bell pepper, baby corn, and shiitake mushrooms and stir-fry for three minutes.

3   Add the choy sum leaves and stir-fry for one minute. Return the cashews and tofu to the wok with the chili sauce and stir together.

4   In a small bowl, mix together the light soy sauce, oyster sauce, cornstarch, and vegetable broth until smooth, and pour into the wok. Stir over a medium heat until the sauce is bubbling, then simmer for one minute and serve immediately.

CHINA

STIR-FRIED CHICKEN WITH SPINACH

SERVES 2 • MARINATING: 3–4 HOURS • PREPARATION: 20 MINUTES
COOKING: 10–11 MINUTES

**2 chicken breasts,
  skinned and cut into
  bite-size pieces
2 tbsp hoi sin sauce
1 tbsp rice vinegar
1 garlic clove, peeled
  and chopped
1 tsp fresh ginger puree
1 tbsp peanut oil
1 red bell pepper, seeded
  and sliced
1 stick of celery, sliced
1 carrot, sliced thin
5 oz baby spinach leaves
Few drops of sesame oil**

Marinate the chicken for longer if you have time so it absorbs plenty of flavor. Pork could be used instead of chicken if you prefer.

1 Place the chicken in a bowl. Mix together the hoi sin sauce, rice vinegar, garlic, ginger, and one tablespoon of water and pour over the chicken, stirring until the pieces are coated. Cover and leave to marinate for three to four hours.

2 Drain the chicken, reserving the marinade. Heat the peanut oil in a wok, add the red bell pepper, celery, and carrot and stir-fry over a medium heat for four minutes. Remove from the wok and set aside.

3 Turn up the heat and when the wok is really hot, add the chicken and stir-fry for three minutes. Lower the heat to medium, return the red bell pepper, celery, and carrot to the wok.

4 Add the spinach and reserved marinade and toss together for three to four minutes until everything is piping hot and the spinach has wilted. Drizzle over the sesame oil and serve.

INDEX

INDEX